Blooming Where
You're Planted

Blooming Where You're Planted

—

52 Prophetic Words for Being Fruitful In and Out of Season

Emily-Rose Lewis
Illustrated by: David Allen Lewis

ISBN-13: 9781545591321
ISBN-10: 1545591326

To Dave, my husband and dearest friend. You are my knight in shining armor, battling and slaying dragons by my side. Thank you for all of the sacrifices you make. I adore you and praise God for sending you to find me.

One

There has been a lot of kicking and screaming along the way as you thrash about in doubt and unbelief about My plans as they unfold before you, but you are moving hesitantly forward in spite of the waves of fear that smack you down on occasion. I am proud of you. Your dreams have been filtered through My mind. Those that serve only to show you the roots of fear that still grip your soul, and torment your mind, are coming into the light; I am defusing them of their power over you. I know that all of the things I have promised you, that have yet to materialize, sometimes make you feel as if I have played a cruel joke on you, but in My assessment you have arrived.

Some days you receive My promises as facts. On those days you feel My Presence palpably. On other days, you are so concerned with the reality of your situation that you forget that truth trumps reality.

There is never a time that I am not hovering over your circumstances creating something beautiful, something virtuous, and something that I will use to glorify Myself through your life. You have been waiting for a miracle, and I do have a miracle in store for you. The miracle that you have been waiting for is fulfilled when you keep your faith in Me regardless of the circumstances that are laughing in the face of all that you have been holding onto.

You are the miracle that I have created today. It is through you that I intend to bring miraculous transformation into your situation. Your faithfulness, your trust, and the hope that you hold onto are the avenues by which My miracle working power will travel.

You need to understand, I am not constrained by time as you are. I see the beginning from the end. I know that what you are experiencing right now is a necessary step for you to move into all that I have for you, into the fullness of My promise. Please do not abort the process through self-pity and unbelief. The head is cresting, the birth canal is open. I need you to push. Breathe deeply. Concentrate. Push.

I'll say it again- now is the time to push. Do not give up. Do not turn back. Do not despair. Do not wallow in self-pity; the time is near. I know your heart cries out for justice, and at times you question whether or not I am even concerning myself with what appears to be the destruction of your dreams being realized, the delay your heart being cherished, and the fulfillment of what I have promised you.

What you do not see is the spiritual forces of darkness screeching and grasping with one final effort to destroy the birth of what you have carried in prayer and weeping, through nights of torment, days of joyful expectation, and days when all your hopes seemed dashed upon the rocks of delay.

I am greater. I am bigger. I am more powerful than all the forces of darkness. All of the mistakes in the recesses of your life and the lives of those that are intricately connected to you will not stop the birth of My promises to you. Please hear Me when I say, the child is not breach. Things are not coming out backwards. There is no deformity. There is no complication. What you are experiencing right now is the birthing process, and you must push. No more second-guessing if what you are experiencing is the pain of childbirth. When the baby is born you will hold the perfect promise in your arms, and you will be prepared to nourish, protect, and take responsibility for the precious life that I have given you: body, soul, and spirit.

This is not to say that there will be no more effort on your part, but the time is coming, and is very near, when you will hold in your arms and behold the beauty on the face of the fulfillment of My promise. You will know beyond a shadow of a doubt where your obedience has led you and will be ready to raise up to full maturity what I have created through your faith in Me.

Revelations 22:13; Genesis 1:2; Galatians 4:19

Two

11/21

The day of rejoicing is at hand. There have been unexpected disappointments that hit you hard as you moved forward in what you rightfully believe to be My will for you. I know your faith has floundered, and for moments you have doubted My goodness for allowing your heart to be crushed, once again, when you had trusted so humbly in My hand of guidance to protect you. It seemed to you that you were left uncovered and uncared for, and still now your faith is a little wobbly as you seek to regain your balance after having been knocked off your feet.

I have not left your side and your angels have been stationed to your right and to your left through the whole ordeal. I not only have your back, but I have you covered from every angle: spiritually, physically, and mentally.

I am the Master Creator. I know exactly what it is that I am bringing forth as I spin you, and your life, on My Potter's wheel. I am shaping you and molding you through your situation into something magnificent and powerful.

What caused you to unravel and even brought you to the point of momentary wrath? My instructions to refrain from anger and turn from wrath, to not fret, were to keep your foot from slipping. <u>It was not the circumstance that caused you to stumble but the way that you reacted.</u>

I am not mad at you. I am not disappointed. I am deeply concerned for your well-being and am here to carry you when you cry out to Me for help. Much of what you are walking through right now is to dig out deeply held misconceptions that you have held about yourself. I am putting to death, once and for all, the lies the enemy has engrained into your heart about your true identity. The next level of authority I am walking you into has no room for the miscalculations of your worth and value, beauty and power, and the call I have placed on your life and the vision I have given you to fulfill it.

Allow Me to reveal you to others in My own time. Remember My Words, 'For those who exalt themselves will be humbled, and those who humble themselves will be exalted.' Go ahead and take the seat of lesser honor and trust that, at the appointed time, I will exalt you.

I am not asking that you drop your shoulders and shuffle through life with false humility or with the belief that I would have you be victimized. I only ask that you keep your eyes on Me and allow Me to release and give you when, where, and how I see fit.

You are My instrument; let Me make music through you. Sometimes you will be the melody of heaven that is a beacon of light from a distance. When I call you away from a situation or person, trust that I know what I am doing. Come away with Me. If you cling, when I say release, it is not love. The music of your life becomes a clanging cymbal. If I do not ask for you to give your body to the flames, and yet you stay and burn, it profits you nothing. Let Me fine-tune you so that the sound of your life will be always sweet and never a bitter clamor for control.

You need a time of refreshing, a time to connect with Me, and a space away to hear Me call your name and remind you of who you are. Take My hand and come with Me. I have a surprise for you! Listen carefully as I direct you away from the voices that are tearing you down, the circumstances that seem to indicate your deepest hearts desires are being thwarted, and the fear that what will be, will resemble what was.

I have given you the power of life and death. It is in the power of your tongue. Dare to speak and create using My Words and thoughts that I release into you by My Spirit. You are more than enough because I am more than enough, and I live in you. You do not need others to immediately line up and recognize what I am doing in and through you. I am more concerned that you believe what I have said about you and what I have said I will do through you. Once you come to a place where you truly believe the Words I have spoken about you it will break the membrane of self-doubt that your identity has been cocooned in; who you have become will be clearly seen.

Do not fight against the pressure. You are complete. Struggle only to free yourself of the useless doubt and fear.

Deuteronomy 31:6; Isaiah 64:8; Psalm 37:8;
Matthew 23:12; Acts 9:15; Proverbs 18:21

Three

You are no longer a slave. You are My child and not only My child, but an heir. You are to share in your Father's estate; you are entitled to an inheritance in My Kingdom. You have shared in My suffering, and you will also share in My glory. Pay no mind to those people that are coming against you as if they have the power to remove you from the place where I have called you. They are but pawns in My hand. You will come in and go out and nothing will touch you; not one hair on your head will be harmed. Though others gnash their teeth at you, belittle you, and seek to convince you that they have control over the direction of your life, I am. With one breath from My mouth I will freeze them in their tracks. Their hand is not long enough to reach across the distance I have removed them from you. Because I live in you, and My angels surround you, no arm can reach you to choke out the life I have given you or hold you back. I have called you to come up into the heights of the mountains with Me. Pay no attention to those that still make their living in the demon possessed valley. Your reward and compensation comes from Me.

At the core of who I made you, lies a strength that you are only now beginning to tap into. I have infused power into your DNA, the seeds of your unique characteristics, to take on every plan the enemy has formed against you with determined ease.

Look up, your help comes from Me. I am the Maker of heaven and earth. In the story I am writing, you are the victor, the undefeated one, the one called holy and blessed, prosperous and influential. Do not be fooled. Wherever you go, and whatever relationships you are in, it is you that brings the change. Do not let others intimidate you with their taunting attitudes of superiority. It is a ruse to cover up for the inadequacy they feel when in your presence. They lack the humility to defer to the truth that you bring to the table. Pay them no mind.

You may wonder about the probability of having the faith to move past the feelings that are stirred by their grappling for power. Look at My face. Do you see My forehead furrowed with worry? Ha! It will never be. I put kings in power and removed them with a flick of My hand. No man can stand before Me save the one I have given the power to do so. Anyone that sets their face against you does so to their own detriment. Do not fear them. Pray they will come to their senses through the discipline that I will be doling out for their self-serving motives. To act as the world acts, reason as the world reasons, and treat you, My friend, as the world treated Me, is to make themselves My enemy. I have clearly stated, those that want to be a friend of the world make themselves

My enemy. Vengeance is Mine. I am a God of justice. Pray for them.

Now, refocus your attention away from the smoke screen and ashes. I have called you to walk in light and beauty. None of these pointless schemes the enemy has brought against you will come to anything. I am using them as a stepping stone to move you into the next level of service and provisioning I have for you.

You will no longer work for human compensation. You will go in and plunder the wealth of the land of promise you have inherited through much tribulation and warfare. Take a look around you. Wherever you see Me place My stamp of promise on a new territory, step forward and claim it as your very own possession.

Shake the dust from your feet as you walk away from the houses of those that refuse to recognize who I am in you, welcome you, or listen to your words. Step into the greater things that I have for you. Now is the time.

Galatians 4:7; 1 Peter 1:4; Revelation 22:12; Psalm 121:2; James 4:4; Deuteronomy 32:35; 1 John 1:7; Colossians 3:23; Matthew 10:14

Four

I know that you have believed Me for above and beyond transformation and blessing and felt let down by the evidence that makes things appear as though only meager efforts on My part have been made to meet you at your level of faith. You hope on against all odds, imagining abundance to the point of overflow, and instead it often seems like the results of your faith and prayers have been a second-rate substitute, or meager portion, of what you had believed would finally bring the confirmation of your belief in My faithfulness to respond to the cry of your heart.

You carry the burden of dashed hopes, heartsick and wandering when I will ever come through for you in such a way that you can breathe again with no dread of evil. The night has been long. The pain has come in waves, great and mighty to smack against the rock in an effort to shake the foundation of your hearts longing. You have groaned in agony, and complained in frustration, but have not been moved. You lift your eyes to the hills, knowing you have a God that has promised to help you but wondering why the journey has been so long and the process so arduous. Will there ever be a season free from enemy attacks from within your own camp you wonder. You want to lie down and sleep in peace every night, to wake each morning with the bright light of a new day dawning and know your life is safe and that those things you cherish, and your yet unfulfilled hopes, will not be ripped to shreds before your very eyes.

For days, and often weeks, you find respite for your soul in contentment and joy only to be swept back into the current of devastation with one firm punch from the enemy's fist. You cry out for mercy. You cry out for help. You believe for specific growth to push through with the expectation you can regain your footing and find ease for the ache of your heart. How many times can ones' hope be deferred you ask Me. You want to believe Me, that the desires of your heart will be fulfilled, but often feel like the blessings are eking out a drop at a time and your thirst is never quenched.

What you must come to more fully understand is that My love gushes and flows forth from the cross in monsoon measures. My faithfulness stretches across the skies and rains down on you night and day. My Spirit is the river that never runs dry. That you still perceive lack, and have the dread of evil, points to your leaning on your own, and others sufficiency, instead of drawing strength from the all-sufficient storehouse of My great Love for you. The doors of heaven have not closed. Why the aching heart? Why the doubt and unbelief? The perceived failure, loss, and defeat of days gone by are no reflection of where I am leading you.

Open your hand. Trust Me with all of your heart. What you are seeing as Me giving you only crumbs to eat, is being seen through the misapprehensions of a divided heart. A servant is not greater than His Master. As it was with Me on earth, so it is with you. Those crumbs are merely falling to the ground before your vision as I break the bread of your life to feed others!

Those crumbs are not the feast I have prepared for you. Look closer. Look again. And again. And again. I have set a table before you in the presence of your enemies. That is the only reason they are still within your view. I desire that they watch as you eat all I have prepared for you.

I want you to be able to say without hesitation, "I have been crucified with Christ and it is no longer I that live, but Christ lives in me. The life I now live in the body, I live by faith in the Son of God, who loved me and gave himself for me."

I made a public spectacle of the powers and authorities of darkness by triumphing over them on the cross. Walk with Me in victory. Let those that doubt My resurrection, and its power to save, see your scars and reach out their hands to touch your gapping wounds; let them see how death has no power over you. My life in you will cause many to stop doubting and believe.

Psalm 3:5, 23:5, 36:5; 2 Corinthians 9:8; John 15:20;
Colossians 2:15; Revelations 20:6

Five

I am giving you an overflow of revelation into the process through which I am answering your prayers. Let the insight that I am raining down from heaven shore up your faith and anchor your heart in hope. Not one detail is being overlooked by My omniscient mind. The depths of My understanding goes down into every crevice of the matters that concern you.

Though My image in the hearts and minds of My chosen ones have been marred by the effects of sin, My plan of redemption includes total restoration. This is what I do, create humans in My image.

There is no plan the enemy has to keep your prayers from being answered that can stop My hand from moving. What you see as a setback or defeat, I see as an opportunity to make what was hidden in deception come forth into the light and be diffused of its power to tempt or destroy. I am removing those things that do not reflect My nature.

You are not to panic when the weight from the revelation of enemies plans hit. I have the victory. In Me you have the victory. Do not consider the time as if you have lost something; your times are in My hands.

Do not give into the worry and anxiety that seeks entrance through thoughts that believe there has somehow been ground lost. No ground has been lost. There is a constant forward progression taking place in those things you have been trusting Me to accomplish. No ground has been lost. You have only been shown where My victory has yet to be applied. My light is shining to expose the works of darkness, and My breath is going out from My mouth to blow them away.

There has been no ground lost.

Hebrews 6:19; Genesis 1:26; Ephesians 5:13; Isaiah 59:19

Six

Draw near to Me, and I will draw near to you. Give me your attention. Remove your misplaced expectations towards others, and place all your expectations on Me. I alone know what it is you need at any given time, and I have promised to meet all of your needs.

There is nothing in this world that will fill the void I created in you. I created you for Myself, and it is in Me alone that you will find rest. The deepest longing of your heart is to be with Me. In intimate relationship, and abiding with Me, you will have passionate, lasting satisfaction for your souls.

Come to Me with a thankful heart. Your attitude of gratitude will peel the scales from your eyes, and you will see Me in the midst of your trials. I am near to you always; in all things I never leave your side. I stand beside you watching your fruitless search for life outside of Me. I am with you in all things. I know your inner thoughts and am there with you as you seek solace and love apart from Me. It hurts My heart to watch you groping around in the darkness for something to latch onto, something that will relieve the ache of your brokenness.

Time and time again you return to broken cisterns for a drink to quench your endless thirst. Why do you refuse to come to Me and drink? I will give you living water. Drink the water I will give you, and you will never thirst again. You chase after the best this world has to offer, seeking excitement, never comprehending the path I call you to walk is the ultimate adventure. The story that I am writing is the only story worth spending your life for. Do you believe that I know what I created you for? Will you believe that I have written a part for you in My story that far surpasses your fumbling efforts to make a life for yourself?

You hold on to your life and in the process lose, not only your life, but your very self. Do you know that apart from Me you can do nothing? Give up! Give up seeking solace in worldly pleasures. They are fleeting and bring no lasting satisfaction. Each compromise draws you further from yourself, further away from Me. I promise to provide pleasures and to satisfy your souls with good things from My overflowing storehouse of blessings. My supply never runs dry.

I created you. I placed specific desires within your heart. I alone am the way to fulfill those deep desires. Follow Me, and I will lead you. Drop your defenses. Abandon your pointless plans, they will only lead to your destruction. Pray for an increase of faith and for healing from the misconceptions about Me you have held for far too long.

I am good. I am love. I have your best interests at heart. Believe My words, obey My words, and you will find the life you long for.

James 4:8; Isaiah 43:21; Psalm 145:18; Jeremiah 2:13;
John 4:13-14; Luke 17:33; Psalm 16:11

Seven

Delight yourself in Me, and I will give you the desires of your heart. Ask and it will be given to you; seek and you will find; knock and the door will be open. You have read My Words correctly. They represent absolute truths, universal laws I have set into motion. For everyone who asks receives; the one who seeks finds; and to the one who knocks, the door will be opened. 'For everyone.' You are a part of this every one of whom I speak.

Do you have the desires of your heart being manifested in the natural and spiritual realm? Are you experiencing the abundant life that I sent My Son to die for you to have? Do you imagine I am the reason why you are experiencing some lack, that somehow I am holding out on you or that you must beg and plead to convince Me to move on your behalf?

I absolutely honor persistence in prayer, but take no pleasure in My children's desperate unbelief that accompanies many of their cries to Me for help. Ask for what you need in faith with no opinion as to how, when, and through whom I will answer, and go about your day in confident assurance, praising Me for My tender care in the preparation of your answer's release.

My whole nature is to give; I created you as an object of My mercy. I am not judging you, weighing your worthiness to receive My good gifts. Let us settle the matter. The only righteousness you have is through your faith in My Son. Do you have faith in My Son? Do you believe that His sacrifice for your sin is complete? Then why beg and plead with Me to meet your needs? Am I standing aloof refusing good things to you? Certainly not!

Fear does not come from Me. Fear has to do with punishment. Banish all fear. On the cross My wrath was satisfied. You have nothing to fear.

Fear not! This is not a suggestion, but a command.

I am a good Father. Will you trust Me to plan out the details of your unfolding life? Can I have the driver's seat? Take your hands off the wheel and relax in the knowledge that I know where I am taking you and the way to get there.

I am the Way.

Psalm 37:4; Mathew 7:7-8; Romans 3:22, 9:23; 1 John 4:18 John 14:6

Eight

11/28/17
pm.

Do not hold back your faith in My power now. You have come so far and suffered much in order to please Me and fulfill the call on Your life. Everything is going to work out. Leave that which concerns you in My capable hands. You are blessed and highly favored. I am moving on your behalf to bring about an outcome far greater than your limited understanding can now comprehend.

Right now, as I speak, I am changing the hearts and minds of those that I have called to support you in your mission on the earth. The hearts of kings are in My hand. I will give you favor with the right people and remove the wrong ones. Let those I remove go without a backward glance. It is My protection of you to remove them. You have armed guards. You are not being rejected. It is not only for your protection, but for theirs, when their hearts turn aside. I have commanded, 'Touch not the Lord's anointed.'

I have been working without ceasing to answer all of your faith filled prayers. Surely you know that I love you far more than you can imagine or comprehend. Speak to your mountain; tell it to move. I gave you My Spirit and My Words. Nothing is impossible to those that believe.

I am provisioning you with the people that have exactly what you need. Everything you need for this day is being provided. Stay your mind on Me and on what I have placed in front of you.

Receive My peace and joy. Leave yesterday and tomorrow in My hands. All the events in your life: years, months, weeks and days are being fashioned by My omnipotent mind to prepare you for the good that I have for you and the good I will do through you.

Rise above the limited mindset that refuses to see My hand of grace moving through the painful circumstances I have allowed you to walk through. You are not being harmed. You are safe in My hands.

Be on the lookout; I am going to whisk you away on an adventure with one of your favorite people. I knew what you would go through ahead of time and have prepared this excursion to ease your troubled mind. I have nothing but good thoughts towards you.

Stick with Me sweetheart, and let Me love on you. Do not worry right now about loving on the ones that have hurt you. They have erred grievously against Me and crushed you. Give your heart to Me today; let Me mend it and treat it with the tenderest of care.

You are blessed and highly favored, called and chosen, set apart and made holy by the blood of the Lamb. You have everything you need in Me.

Luke 1:28; Psalm 105:15; Mark 11:23-24;
Hebrew 10:10

Nine

Do not ignore emotional pain when it grips your heart; pain is a symptom of injury. I am the Great Physician. Do you believe that I desire to heal you? Do you believe I love those you love even more than you do and desire that they be healed and delivered too?

Just as you would make an appointment, and rearrange your schedule, to visit a physician when you have a physical injury or illness and the symptoms persist, so you must learn to schedule extra time with Me, the Great Physician, to receive the diagnosis, prescription, and instructions I have for you that will lead to yours or your loved ones' healing.

If a doctor ordered nothing by mouth prior to a surgery would you plow ahead and eat a big meal? By no means! Neither should you ignore My leading to refrain from food when it comes. Often a time of fasting is needed to prepare the way for My healing touch. If you knew how many healings were not received simply because an intercessor ignored My call to lay aside food, you would never again consider it a small thing to serve your bellies over Me.

Just as you would go out of your way to take an ailing loved one to see a specialist when their bodies are failing, in spiritual matters, you must be willing to bring the wounds and burdens of others to Me. In My Presence, listening to My voice, I will lead you into all truth. Ask Me to reveal the source of your pain; I will. When you begin to understand the root of the symptoms of your pain, you can then ask Me for what you want specifically. I desire an intimate friendship with you. Take time with Me, and we will discuss My plans for healing and redemption.

Do not be afraid of pain. Pain is only temporary. I am able to do amazing things for, and through you, as you begin to understand the benefits of paying attention to what your pain is trying to show you.

Some things I am able to heal instantly because of the great faith of the one that requests. Other ills require following My specific instructions and the passage of time. Spend time with Me, and your faith will grow.

I understand that some wounds are deep and festering with decay from years of neglect and running. Many addictions are formed by those seeking relief from their pain. In seeking shelter elsewhere, and in detaching from one's heart through addiction, pain can be temporarily numbed. Addiction is just a modern word for idolatry. Until one is willing to recognize that something is terribly wrong, and come to understand it is only in Me that things can be made right, their soul will remain fractured.

It is not My will for My children to live with a spirit of heaviness and grief always looming over their life. If darkness and suffering have become your constant companions, I desire to set you free, but you must ask Me in faith, believing that I am able to deliver you.

As I was on the earth, so am I now in you. Ask and you will receive. Listen to My voice and believe Me. By obeying My specific instructions you will experience the victory I secured for you on the cross in your own heart and in the hearts of those that I have given you.

Psalm 103:3; Matthew 7:7, 17:21; John 16:13

Ten

It is time to stop looking back in longing at that relationship that I have declared is dead in your life. It is not, and will never again be, what I am using to bring you into your inheritance and destiny. Yes, I ordained that relationship for you, but it was for a season, and that season has past. Let the dead bury their own dead; you must come and follow Me.

Give me your fickle hearted attention as an act of faith, and allow Me to help you fix your eyes on what is before you. What is ahead is far better than what lies behind you. Can you see that what has happened was to move you out of a place of stagnation and off of a path that twists and turns and is often hidden from view as to where your next step will lead you? Be glad that you are now aware that had I not gone before you to make your path straight you would have had your foot caught indefinitely in the snare of the way of strife, confusion, fear, and resistance to My ways.

You did not ruin your chances. What was is not My best for you. Regret is only useful in so far as you learn from your mistakes the lessons I intended for you to learn to prepare you for the next thing. In living in regret you miss the point of the whole thing and languish in the memories of yesterday instead of applying the lessons born from your pain to today's circumstances.

Regrets are just lessons waiting to be learned.

You cannot turn back time, but you can sabotage today's blessing when you refuse to allow Me to fully heal your heart by not letting go of those things that are behind. Stop picking at the scab with your backward glances and longings. Have you forgotten so easily what things were really like?

Intensity of emotion does not always equal the value of that emotion.

Allow me to lead you beside the bubbling brook of relational fulfillment that does not run dry. Let me cause the fires of your passion to burn brightly without blowing up in your face or burning out. Set your affections on Me and those that I have clearly set before you on your journey with Me. Lay aside all of your preconceived ideas about who I intend to use to answer your prayers. You have learned that your fear and opinions about My ways can negatively affect outcomes in your life and relationships. Break the pattern. Trust Me to orchestrate your deliverance.

Your part is to concern yourself with My business in the lives of those I have given you. Let your life be the fulfillment of their hearts' desires. Take no thought for your own needs fulfillment. I will fill you to overflow as you pour out your life for My purposes to be accomplished. Do not be afraid to love. Freely you have received, freely you are to give, without condition. Follow Me.

Leave the past in the past, and your dreams will be sweetened by the fragrance of your surrender.

Matthew 10:8; Luke 9:60; Philippians 3:13

Eleven

Do not fret over the details about what is going on internally in the areas that I am healing in your life and the lives of the ones that are close to your heart. Trust in the process that is taking place in your relationships. Circumcision of the heart is a painful process, and the healing does not happen overnight. Do not try to force intimacy. Refrain from anger and turn from wrath. Do not fret and worry. Be patient and stand in faith. The circumcision of a heart is My work and My responsibility.

I have called you to love. Do not needily grope or grovel. You are My child, a royal heir. Bow your knee only to Me. Fear only Me. Put your faith fully in my ability to cut away all the fleshly and soulish rubbish of the past. The occasional pain, awkwardness, and distance you feel are all necessary. These are the ramifications of the surgery I am performing.

Do not get caught in the trap of performance anxiety, believing yourself to be My only useful scalpel or healing balm. When you feel panicked by an attack on your mind of racing thoughts, trying to find an immediate solution to untangle the issues you face, pause and remember, I AM. I am the Author and the Finisher of your faith; I am working all things for good. Your life is precious to Me. You are but one part of a whole. I have a plan that encompasses not only working out the details of your life for your greatest good, and My glory, but to bring into glory those that I am using you to fashion into My likeness. When you begin to wonder what you can do to fix what appears to be broken, look within. Let the discomfort you are experiencing point you to an area in your own heart that needs My touch.

Am I enough for you? Do My promises bolster your faith to keep your eye on the prize and follow My leading through, and out of, every difficulty that you are facing? My child, what is needed is a peaceful and gentle spirit; a safe oasis for others to experience My Presence.

Do you long for the day when your deepest needs for intimacy will be met? There is no greater desire of My heart than to be intimately connected with you and give you the pleasure of our unions fulfillment. There is no human relationship that can permanently delete the ache in your heart. Your deepest desires will only be completely fulfilled when I bring you home to be with Me in heaven, your true home. In the meantime, I am creating a space in your mind, will, and emotions devoid of the clamor of the world's faulty system of interpreting circumstances and relationships where My Spirit can be comfortable and interpret things for you.

Cooperate with Me. Co-create with Me. Slow and steady dear one. Take the long view of things. Are you in this for the long haul? Why the hurry? All things in My perfect timing. Celebrate the small victories. Do not focus on the disappointments. Let them roll off your back like the victor that you are. Shrug it off and move on. Let your hope rest on Me and in the knowledge I know what your needs are. I am meeting them. Draw on our intimacy to meet your deepest needs and then turn right around and give the unmerited grace and favor I give you away.

Watch Me transform you. I will make light shine through you into the darkest recess of your situation and perform a circumcision of heart that will never be reversed. The final outcome will look nothing like the beginning.

Romans 2:28-29, 8:28; Hebrews 12:2; Ecclesiastes 3:1

Twelve

I have called you by name. My hand of favor has been stretched out to you. The time of salvation is at hand. Give Me all that you are and all that you have. Surrender every last detail of your hopes and desires, dreams and visions, preferences and repulsions.

I want you to relinquish control over your entire life: the good, the bad, the ugly, as well as the parts that you believe are useful and of value for My purposes. All of your preconceived ideas as to how I intend to use you must be completely and utterly relinquished. Lay them all at the foot of the cross. Come to Me with empty hands. I will fill you up with the substances of heaven that are vastly superior to what must die to be reborn into the above and beyond life that My mind has conceived for you.

Your finite mind cannot begin to imagine what I am capable of doing through the life of someone that is willing to eradicate self-will and join their heart and mind with Mine through passionate yielding to the impulse of My love in all things.

There is no room on this path of magnificent fulfillment for half-hearted believers. To receive everything that I have for you, you must not love the world or anything in the world. The craving for physical pleasure, a craving for everything you see, and pride in your achievements or possessions, do not come from Me. Will you serve Me if you are striped of those things that hold value in the eyes of the world and the hope of attaining those things you have longed for?

Through My wise and loving discipline I will purge from your heart and life twisted desires that lead to death and false motives to accomplish even your noble pursuits.

I will weigh all things by My measure of justice and place everything in its proper place. I have created you with specific calculations to fit the place I have made for you in the story I am writing through your life. Those ambitions that are useless to fit the DNA of your journey will be burned in the fires that you walk through if you will hold steady in the flames.

There is no one exactly like you. The specifications of your adventure have been planned down to the last detail, with careful consideration being given to every injustice doled out to you at the hands of those that have refused to live out the purpose for which they were created, those that surrendered their lives to the power of darkness to wreak havoc in the hearts of My chosen people.

The calling that was placed on you at birth, to be an integral part of My redemptive plan in the earth during this moment in history, was recognized by the forces of evil. A plan was hatched to steal from you the seeds of greatness that I had planted within you by My hand of favor. The gift of free will that

I gave humanity was perverted and caused you great harm. Abandon your will totally to Me and watch in amazement what I can do to turn around the destruction caused by the will in rebellion.

What may appear to have been wasted years, I call vital chapters to the story of your life. The odds were stacked against you. The ruination seemed complete, but in My infinite wisdom I chose you from among the people to expose the darkness and reveal My glory through the brokenness of your life. The stain of sin that you were crushed under for so long is going to be used as ink in My pen to write the future chapters of your life.

Could anyone that has not experienced depravity as you have ever appreciate as you will the majesty of My holiness flowing to and through them? My answer is no.

I will redeem all that you have suffered, both at the hands of others and by your own hands that were tied. I will remove the ancient stones, tear up the weeds that choked out new life, and build within your heart a heavenly garden, a Spirit created space, where the light will never burn out and the plants will never whither. Your life will be a source of refreshing where rivers of living water will flow, to and through you, to those I bring along your path. All that come into contact with you will see My hand of favor on your life. You will have honor among those that long to know Me, and you will be hated by those that hate Me.

You will reflect a unique facet of My beauty and strength into the world around you.

Every step you take will be motivated by My love. I will restore to you purified those desires that had been distorted by the festering wounds of what was.

I will be able to trust you with far more provision than you could have handled prior to the surrender. You will stand in awe at all I have done, but be no more affected by the abundance that I pour into your lap than if I had continued to withhold what you were not ready to receive. I will teach you the secret of being content in all things. Because you will have given Me all that you had, including those things you held as precious and good, I will be able to trust you to be a conduit of My extravagant grace, both in the spiritual and material realms.

Check your life. Release whatever is in your hands, even if you believe it is being held for safe keeping. Nothing that you withhold from Me is safe. Even those things that are most lovely and admirable, if you are unwilling to part with them, will block the flow of My life. I will return to you whatever is needed: when, how, and where I see fit, having transformed it into the exact etching of what your heart's truest longing is for. Be prepared to say goodbye forever to it all, knowing what you lose for My sake and the sake of the gospel will be multiplied back to you 100 times.

Release it all. I have set you free!

Isaiah 43:1; 1 John 2:15-16; Jeremiah 29:11;
Zephaniah 3:19; John 7:38; Philippians 4:12-13

Thirteen

12/12/17

I have given you power. Within you resides the power to have an abundant life. What you choose to focus your attention on will be magnified in its power over you. Focus your attention on Me, the only safe option. Anything else that you allow to control you, will destroy you. When you fix your eyes on the unseen realm, instead of staring at the painful circumstances or lack that you are experiencing in the natural realm, you will find that abundance is the truth.

I understand the way you feel when you are in agonizing pain at the hands of those who do not recognize who you are or understand what they do and know you sometimes wonder where I am in the midst of it all. I will show you the way if you will follow Me.

 Yes, there is a time to mourn, but there is also a time to dance. Rise up by putting a song of praise in your heart and My Words in your mouth. Stand firm in the liberty I give you by setting your mind on My Spirit; it will bring life and peace to you.

Train your mind not to settle around the issues in your life that you are believing Me to change.

As a foreman studies the construction plans and gathers the building materials to prepare for creating what has been given to him in blueprints, so should you dig into My Word and apply it to your life. Why stand beside the half-finished project wailing that you do not have all that you need to finish? Did you not consider the cost of following Me, as I instructed, before you set to work? It will cost you everything. If you have lack, it is not on My end. What are you holding back from Me? I am the One that created the blue print for your life, and it is I that have promised to be the Author and the Finisher of your faith. I have given you everything you need to complete the project I designed. I will provide every tool, every material, and every helper that is needed.

If you are focusing your attention on point A, instead of on Me, you can miss hearing Me say what you need is at point B. Keep moving forward towards Me in love and trust.

At times you are unable to receive what you need for the next step of the project because your hands are full of the stuff of life I have told you to take your hands off of. Let it go in order to receive from Me. I assure you, none of the lack you are experiencing is from My hands. I give life abundant and everything that is needed to accomplish all that I have commissioned you to do.

Check the blueprint, make sure it is My Word. Check the foundation, make sure it is My life. Check your life, make sure you are holding nothing back. Your pain does not come from Me.

> Colossians 3:2; Ecclesiastes 3:4; Galatians 5:1;
> Luke 14:28; John 10:10

Fourteen

12/12/17

I am working on your relational situation to bring about an outcome that is far better than your limited understanding can comprehend at this time. This is why I am not unveiling all the details to you. Your part is to trust Me, obey Me, and to go to war through prayer and fasting. Stop believing that you have to wrestle with Me to release your blessing. Yes, I am calling you to wrestle, but you are wrestling the blessing I have already released on your behalf from the hands of the enemy and those things that would hinder what is already loosed in heaven from manifesting on the earth.

Do not ignore My explicit instructions to shut out all distractions and focus on the task at hand. Do not look for the manna from heaven that I have been using to feed you in the last season anymore, it will never be again. You are entering into your promised land flowing with milk and honey!

Now is the time to take possession of the land.

You have been tested and tried in the last season. You now recognize that your ungratefulness, grumbling, pride, and unbelief are offensive to Me and have no place in your future. Do not resist this time of uncertainty. You can be certain of Me and My desire to bring you into your inheritance.

I have stripped you down to lighten the load for battle. Today you must rise up and take possession of your miracle. I have released it already. No need to ask of Me anymore for what I have already promised is yours. Get up. March. Shout songs of praise and deliverance. Pray in My Spirit. Open your mouth and declare the truth over those people and relationships that have been bound, not by My hand, but by the hand of the enemy. Release My people through your intercession.

This is not the time to focus on anything other than My face. Look on My face and you will see a smile of satisfaction as I watch you smear the enemies plans to hold back My provision and blessing. Listen for My voice and you will hear My laughter at the adversaries that rise up against you and your inheritance as My chosen and dearly loved child.

Ephesians 3:20-6:12; Deuteronomy 27:3

Fifteen

Run towards the goals and visions that I have placed in your heart with unflinching faith. I am only placing a bridge under your feet for the next couple of steps in front of you. Do not wait for the waters to dry up, the mountains to be moved, or for an opening in the wall that rises up to block your progress.

Move confidently and joyfully forward. Trust that when you reach the waters, they will dry up or part; when you come to a mountain, it will be cast into the sea or I will give you wings to soar above its heights; the walls that seem to be barriers to your progress will crumble with your shouts of praise, or a door will appear, at the exact moment you are about to be stopped by the blockade.

Sing and praise; use the words of your mouth and the meditation of your heart to co-create with Me all the good things I have in mind to do in and through you. Allow the obstacles and challenges that you encounter to purify your heart and draw you closer to Me. Seek first My kingdom and My righteousness, and ALL of these things will be added to you as well. With every bit of increase sow the first fruits into My Kingdom and watch in amazement as I multiply back to you what your seed, watered by faith in My word, will bring forth in your life.

Give and it will be given.

Bless those that come against you and do not curse them. Trust in my ability to bring justice into your life. Do not expect people to pay you back. I am the keeper of all of your accounts. As you release your enemies in love, I will be released to settle their accounts against you in My way and in My time. Be on the lookout for how I will be restoring to you what has been stolen in this last season. Remain faithful to Me even when you are surrounded by those that are unfaithful.

Give yourself fully to the work of My Kingdom. Know that even in the areas of your life that are unspiritual I am there and want to use you as a container for My glory in the earth. I have placed you in dark places to be a light; a beacon of hope to a lost and dying world. Let My hope fill you as you look to Me to meet all of your needs. Come to Me for refreshing. Rest with Me and be still. Be still and know that I am God. I am the One that meets all of your needs.

Do not neglect to ask Me, even about the small and simple things in your life. Ask Me for wisdom and insight into your dealings. Open your eyes to the varied ways I will be speaking to you the things that you need to hear to be clear about the direction I am leading you in.

One step at a time. One day at a time. March forward with unflinching faith. Mountains will crumble; waters will part; doors will be opened. There is nothing to fear. Laugh

with Me in the face of fear. Bow before Me and your enemies
will bow before you.

1 Corinthians 9:24; Psalm 19:14, 46:10;
Matthew 6:33; James 1:5 Luke 6:28, 6:38; Matthew 5:14

Sixteen

There are some people that simply do not have eyes to see Me as I am, ears to hear My voice when I speak, or a heart that believes the truth when I have made it known. Do not wrap your value up in how others see you, or how they receive what you have said, and do not let your faith in yourself waiver because someone else is unable to believe the truth about you. You are not a second-rate afterthought, a hand-me-down desperate for a second chance, a beggar hoping for a handout to get through the day. Your value far surpasses that of silver and gold; your worth is comparable to My very life. I died for you.

The beauty that I have bestowed on you should never be measured by its ability to produce lust in foul hearts perverted by covetousness. What do unsanctified creatures know about true beauty that radiates from the hearts of one of My chosen ones? Never step out of My radiance to prove yourself to one unable or unwilling to see you as you are, in all the measure of glory that you walk in, reflecting My heart and beauty to the world around you. You have nothing to prove to the fallen nature of man. Allow all things resembling rejection in your life to drive you deeper into My acceptance, knowing that I am working all things for the good of those that love Me and are called according to My purpose, including the decisions of those around them whose walks are faltering at best and faithless at worst.

Why fault a blind man for not being able to recognize your beauty or a deaf man for being unable to receive your words as truth?

Do not allow yourself to fall prey to the trap of the enemy that compels you to make yourself known. I know you. Know yourself. Allow Me to reveal who you are, your beauty and your strength, your heart and your value, to those that I choose and that for My purposes to be fulfilled. Never measure yourself by how you are received by others. How you are received is a measure of others ability to receive, nothing more, nothing less.

Go where I send you without fear. Offer the gifts that I give you to those that I direct you to. Do not be offended when the gift is tossed aside or devalued. What is it to you? Am I not the source of all things good? It is Me that they are rejecting. A servant is not above their Master. Bear the burden bravely and keep your eyes on Me. I am training you so that you will not be susceptible to deception because of the pain associated with rejection. When you are spending ample time in My Presence, allowing Me to heal you from the hits that your perception takes by the fallen perception of others, you will be able to measure yourself in accordance with the faith I have given you.

Ask Me to increase your faith, not only in Me, but in yourself. If no one else in the world valued what you offered them in love and faith, know that you have pleased Me immensely to have exercised the courage I have given you by offering yourself where, when, how, and to whom I have directed you. You are fully accepted and appreciated by Me. Go in peace.

1 Peter 1:18-19; Luke 18:19; Romans 15:7

Seventeen

12/20/17

I am going to bless you in ways that you cannot even now imagine. Yes, you will prosper. Hold nothing back from Me, not now, not when you have more than you could ever need. Give generously. I am making you a stream flowing with life and provision into the lives of others. Do not worry about finances. I've got this!

The fears and anxieties that have blocked the flow of My Spirit to and through you are breaking; the floodgates of heaven are opening over your life. Prepare yourself. Be well balanced in exercise, work, play, and leisure. Take care of your body My strong and beautiful child. There is much that I need you to do, and you will need your body to accomplish My will. Take care of My temple. Feed on Me. Taste and see that I am good. Let your soul delight in the richness of My fare.

Give Me all of your time and I will multiply it and give it back to you. Do not focus on being productive for Me, focus on intimacy with Me, and through our union many will be healed. Do not let the desire for an abundant life fall by the wayside of your vision believing that this is what would please Me. It will please Me for you to have overflow to bless those I send to you with grace and style.

Ask and you shall receive. Seek and you will find. I desire to prosper you in every area of your life, including financially. I know that as you hear My Words you do not completely believe them. You want to but are afraid that they are not My true heart. You are concerned with your desire for wealth, worried that it springs forth from your sin nature. I know you more than you know yourself. I know that you do not love this world or anything in it like you love Me.

Let the glimmer of hope that wants to believe that I desire to prosper you as your soul prospers be fanned into flames by your generosity. If you are faithful in your current level of prosperity, you can be entrusted with greater provisioning by My hand.

It is not pleasing to Me when My children misunderstand My nature and believe it is My will for them to barely scrape by. The Kingdom of Heaven is not about scarcity, but abundance.

Seek first My Kingdom and My righteousness, and All of these things will be added to you as well. These are My words. Believe them.

Malachi 3:10; 1 Peter 5:8-9; Isaiah 55:2;
1 John 2:15; Matthew 6:33

Eighteen

You have not because you ask not. My words are true. What is it that you need? Ask Me. Have you asked and not received? When you ask, you do not receive, because you ask with wrong motives, that you may spend what you get on your own pleasures. Check your motives for asking. I will deny no good thing to those who walk uprightly before Me. When you become completely convinced that I am a loving and good Father that wants only what is best for you, you are freed from the worry and anxiety caused by feeling like you need to plead with Me to meet your needs.

Determine in your heart today to believe in Me and relax in the understanding that I have your best interests always before Me. Resist the temptation to help me out in answering your prayers. All that is necessary is that you seek Me with your whole heart, and cast all of your cares on Me, knowing that I care deeply for you. I sent My son to die for you. Not only to redeem you for Myself, but to take away the sins of the whole world.

Do not fear the consequences of your sin. Any time I bring conviction or correction it is out of love and a desire to help you grow into all the ways that I have called you to walk. I am molding you and making you into the person that I have conceived in My heart. You are a unique and treasured object of My love. You are not an object of My wrath. On the cross, My wrath against all sin, was fully satisfied.

You are under the umbrella of My protection and an object of My mercy. My thoughts are always on how I can do good to and through you. Do not fear fallen humanity and the corruption and decay in the lives of those you encounter. No one else's mistakes or shortcomings can hold you back from the abundant life I died for you to have. Look to the cross. Everything that you need to live a victorious life was accomplished on Calvary.

Hold nothing back from Me, dear one. The only hindrance to all the desires of your heart being fulfilled is your hesitance to fully surrender in all things to Me. I am close to you. There is no distance between us save what you experience when you resist My love. I never leave you, and I will never forsake you. Even when you are faithless, I will remain faithful. The distance you sometimes feel is often manifesting because of your refusal to totally surrender your heart to My safe keeping and your life to My constant guidance.

Your relational experiences have at times caused you to feel the need to build walls of protection around your heart. I understand this completely. Those defenses seemed to you completely necessary for your survival when they were being formed.

Now is the time to move forward in confidence and a deeper understanding of My concern for you. In this season you are now entering those walls and defenses are no longer necessary. You know Me more personally than you did in the past season. The spirit of independence that brought you out must now give way to a spirit of total dependence on My great, sacrificial Love for you.

I love you. I say this with tears in My eyes! I love you. I love you. I love you.

You can trust Me to heal your heart and keep it close to My heart where every attack must first be filtered through My heart of perfect love. I will use ALL things; I will work ALL things for your good.

Do you believe Me? Do you believe that I love you? Then bind yourself in total surrender to this truth and watch Me come through for you and bring you through every circumstance victoriously.

James 4:2-3; Psalm 84:11; 3 John 1:2; 1 Peter 5:7;
John 1:29; 2 Timothy 2:13; Romans 8:28

Nineteen

1/6/18

My word to you today, as it is every day, is 'Abandon.' Throw
yourself fully into My arms of grace and mercy. Run towards
Me and not away from the problem; in pursuit of Me your
problems will be resolved to the exact specification of My
plans for your betterment and highest good. Release yourself
from the bondage created by the illusion that you can control
the outcomes of your decisions, lives, and relationships.

Have you heard My voice saying, 'This is the way,' but
are second guessing yourself endlessly for fear of stepping out
of my perfect will? Get quiet with Me, let Me guide you with
peace and lead you forward with a song of victory in your
heart because you have placed your confidence, not on what
man can do for you, but in what I have promised to accomplish in and through your life. Learn to make decisions and
pad those decisions with your faith in My ability to come
through for you in the most unlikely ways.

A double-minded man is unstable in all his ways.

Have you noticed how on some days you will be going
along your way, perfectly contented and happy, until you

come to a crossroads? You can either choose to see what is before you with a grateful attitude, and in a spirit of grace and confidence, or you can see things through eyes of discouragement, fear, or ungratefulness and discontent.

When you choose faith, and choose confidence in My ability to work through those prayers and the decisions that you have made through prayerful consideration, you choose life and peace. Do not allow the enemy to come in with arguments and reasonings that cause you to second guess yourself and to distrust the processes by which I am working all things for your good and My glory. If you are about to make a grave error, I will send definite and repeated warnings prior to your foot being caught in an irrevocable trap.

Notice when you begin to waffle on your own decisions based on those things in the natural that can easily be used to talk yourself out of moving forward with confidence that I am directing your steps. Fear of future lack is not from Me. Trust Me. Trust yourself to hear My voice. Trust that the decisions you make in faith are not going to destroy the good plan I have for your life or leave you destitute and disillusioned.

I have you! Hold your head up high as one that has been given authority over sin and death, as one anointed to take dominion of the earth. You are not a scraping peasant that need beg Me to help you barely get by. Make your decisions based on

faith in My grace to meet your needs in the future, not just because you always make perfect decisions, but because that is part of My nature, and I have promised you that My grace is sufficient.

Colossians 3:15; James 1:8; Romans 6:14;
2 Corinthians 12:9

Twenty

I see that you have been striving to reach perfection. Know this, in Me you have already been made perfect. Rest in the perfection imparted to you by the finished work of the cross. I am in you, and you are in Me. You are hidden with Me in heavenly places; you have My sufficiency in all that you are and everything you do. Draw on My perfection and you will see it being made complete through your natural life.

There is no obstacle, no sin, no fear, no doubt, no lack, no trespass, no insufficiency in My life, and you have died, and My life is being manifested through you. Rise up in My power and in the faith that I have imparted unto you. Ask and it will be given; seek and you will find. Know that in all things, I am working for your good.

Your desire to please Me brings joy to My heart. You are My precious child, and there is nothing or no one that can snatch you out of My hand. You are not subject to the whims of mere mortals. I am the immortal God, and I am still on the throne. Nothing can touch you without first being filtered through My perfect love. Do not tire of hearing Me say this. Believe it. Let it sink deep down into the depths of your being. I am perfect love. I love you perfectly. You are mine. You are under my protection, and there is nothing that can harm you.

You cannot even begin to imagine the magnitude of the tidal wave of blessing that is rushing towards you as we speak. Do you see the waves crashing towards you? Do not fear the waves! They carry with them an anointing of My power and pro-vision like you have never experi-ence before. You will look back on this season as the launching pad of the best years of your life. You have been tested and tried. You have made yourself pli-able in My hands. It is time to be released into greater things; greater measures of abundance in faith, love, joy, peace, provi-sion, and fulfilment of promise are upon you now. You sense it by the very strength you are experiencing in the midst of difficult circumstances. You have entered a new level of glory. Pause and meditate on My perfect love, and peace will flood your heart and mind. You are perfect in My sight. Enjoy the ways that I am working out My perfection in your natural life.

Hebrews 10:14; Ephesians 2:6; Romans 8:28;
Matthew 7:7; Luke 10:19

Twenty-one

1/14/18

Let Me help you see things as I do. I have told you that My ways are higher than your ways, and so they are. I am not confined to time as you are. Time is a created thing. When I look at you, I see perfection. The reality of who you have been, and what you have done, do not trump the truth of who you are in Me. Although your body and mind are bound in time, your spirit is eternal.

From your perspective, you experience process; from My perspective, I experience product. The finished work of the cross is being made complete in your life, and life circumstances, and is also complete already. Cut yourself free from the pressures of the clock. Get an eternal, "It is finished," perspective.

You are My Child! What you will be has not yet been made known in this earth realm, but in the realm of eternity, I see it clearly. There is no sin in Me. My Spirit lives in you, freeing you from the power of sin and death. You have My seed on the inside of you; therefore, you will not go on sinning. You have My love in you; therefore, you will love as I love. Why do you doubt My power to save, purify, and empower you to be as I am?

Have you seen Me? Those that believe in the Son, believe in Me; those that know the Son, know Me; those that love, the Son love Me. If you believe in Me, you will not believe the lies of your circumstances that seek to convince you that I am not good. If you know Me, you know that My heart is to do you good and not evil all the days of your life. And if you believe in, know, and love Me you will hear My voice. Those that hear My voice and follow Me do not recognize a strangers voice and do not follow it.

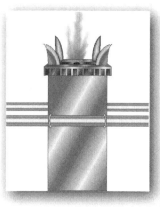

Come away with Me into our secret place and let Me show you who you are in Me. Bear hardship as discipline. Get an eternal perspective. Let the anxiety and fear associated with the boundaries you are experiencing because of what appears incomplete or imperfect 'in time,' roll over onto My shoulders. Let Me expand your view of the eternity I have placed within your heart: eternal perfection and completeness, eternal purity and glory, eternal wholeness and unity. We are one.

Isaiah 55:8; Romans 8:2; 1 John 3:9;
John 10:27, John 14:9, John 17:3, John 19:30

Twenty-two

1/23/18

No more waiting for the fulfillment of that which was promised to you. Today is the day of your salvation. What the enemy has toiled, maneuvered, and manipulated to thwart in your life is not being held back by My hand. Reach out with your arms of faith and take hold of that which is already yours. Not tomorrow, not a week from now, but today. This very day what has been stored up for you is being poured out in abundance over your life. The scales from your eyes are falling off. Your preconceived ideas as to how I would answer the deepest cries of your heart are being removed so that you can perceive My goodness that is already in your midst.

Do not look back. Yesterday is gone. The pain of yesterday is over; feel it no more. Root out any false belief that you owe those things that are now dead your mourning. You owe nothing to anyone except a continued debt of love. Love on. Live on. Move on.

Love endures all things. This is your day to believe that the death you have endured was to build your faith to believe that what I have put in your lap is the beginning of the fulfillment of My promises to you.

I am proud of you and pleased with you. You have learned to follow the signs that I have placed along your path, and My Spirit that I have placed within your heart, with less hesitation. The thoughts that contradict what I have shown you do not hold the power to create fear in you as they once did. Now you are able to walk by faith! Open wide your eyes of faith and take in the scene before you. Do you see the possibilities unfolding before you, the path straightening beneath your feet, and your provision in full view of those beautiful eyes of faith that you now see by, unimpeded by the fear of death?

Feel the bubbling brook of joy and the waves of peace. These are the indicators that what you are believing for you are receiving. Follow joy. Follow peace. Let the dead bury their own dead. No more mourning those things that were brought into your life only to prepare you for this day. Again I say, NOW is the day of salvation. Do not pray, 'Come quickly Lord.' I am here with you already. Pray, "Your Kingdom come, Your will be done." Open your eyes to see the truth of My Kingdom and My will being made manifest in your life.

2 Corinthians 6:2; Romans 13:8; 1 Corinthians 13:7;
Luke 9:60; Matthew 6:10

Twenty-three

In some areas of your life you have felt as if you are just drifting along, carried by the current of circumstances that are beyond your control. In many ways your understanding of your life has been incredibly limited. At times you feel that I have just been allowing you to tread water indefinitely with no real purpose or end in sight.

What you see as drifting, I see as positioning. I have told you before that your circumstances are not random, and indeed they are not. I am proud of you; you have finally stopped thrashing about as if you were drowning and remembered that I am with you in all things. But you are to grow further, past simply recognizing that I am here and still working behind the scenes, into a place where you recognize that each situation, relationship, and trial has been specifically designed to show you something about yourself that you would not have otherwise realized.

Things are beginning to come into focus as you look back and remember how everything that I have walked you through, impurities in your character and imbalances in your life, were brought into the light and dealt with. Turn around and see all the dead weight that has been shed throughout the years. You are not endlessly drifting! You have been afloat on the ocean of My love. With each storm you have sought out those things within your spirit that weigh you down and hold you back and have cast them overboard.

Look behind you. Do you see the trail of useless things floating away on the currents of life as you sail into the sun, light and free? The darkest nights of the soul, the fiercest tempest, have made you brave and strong, recognizing that which no longer serves a purpose in your life and casting it aside. Now, not only do you realize that I am with you, but that I am not asleep in the boat.

All power has been given to Me in heaven and on earth. I am not only with you, I am for you. I have been preparing you for something greater than you can even now imagine.

Can you see now why I have commanded you to rejoice in your sufferings? The hope that you now have cannot be taken from you!

Now prepare yourself, brace yourself, and raise your level of expectation higher than you have dared to raise it before. Coming into your life this year is a flood of blessings, a harvest from the seeds of faithfulness that you have planted and cultivated these long years.

Look around you now, whatever lingering habits, relationships, or activities that are pointlessly taking up space and choking out life, toss them overboard. I declare, today is the day of power to solidify your will against all that clogs the wells of life from springing up within you.

As in the days of Noah, when I caused a flood to rain out of heaven and water to spring forth from the earth to destroy what had been formerly created, so are the floods that have been allowed into your life. Only the relationships and provision that I have ordained for you will be carried into the new life I am creating. I am supernaturally bringing to you those things which you need for success and survival.

You have believed My promises and held tight to the dreams and visions that I have placed within your heart, sacrificing many of the comforts and securities that come from relying, not on Me, but on your own understanding. Your faith will be richly rewarded. Step out of the boat and onto dry land. Receive unimpeded a new life full of grace, provision, favor, creative power, divine connections and relationships, healing power, and fullness of joy.

Matthew 8:26, Matthew 28:18; Romans 5:3;
Proverbs 3:5

Twenty-four

Trust Me, and do not be afraid. Trust in the ability I have given to you to be led by My Spirit. Do not allow doubt and unbelief to cause you to second guess yourself after you have made a decision by My guidance.

✳ The enemy wants to tie your emotions up in knots and riddle you with anxiety by causing you to worry that I am not the one leading you and that the steps you are taking will lead you into failure and defeat. These are lies sent to infiltrate your mind and draw your thoughts away from Me and My plan, from peace.

The moment you feel yourself sinking and second guessing yourself draw away into the secret place of solitude with Me. Even if you only have minutes or moments focus your eyes on the cross and listen as I bring My Word up from your spirit into your mind. Take those words and meditate on them until they calm the waves of worry that threaten My rightful place in your heart.

Do you need conformation that the decision you have made is by My guidance? Ask Me and I will graciously give to you all that you need to walk forward in confidence. I take no delight in seeing My children confused, and taking steps of obedience in fearful reluctance, because they desire to please and follow Me but are afraid of falling into a trap. My Word is a lamp to your feet and a light for your path. You are not walking in darkness anymore. Step out in faith knowing that I will honor your genuine, heartfelt desire to please Me regardless of the possibility that you will take a misstep. Your wobbly steps of obedience cannot mess up the good plan I have for your life.

As you move forward, letting go of what lies behind and pressing towards the good things that are ahead, your sight will improve. With each step of faith you take the path before you will appear brighter; you will gain confidence in Me as you see Me cause all things to work together for your good. There are many things that will remain obscured from your view until the appointed time. I will not reveal them to you until you are ready. Seek My face and not just My hand.

Do you need a sign? Ask for one and then put aside all preconceived ideas of what I plan to do, how I plan to do it, and who I plan to do it through. Watch and wait for Me to confirm the steps you are to take. As you lay aside all of your preferences, My hand will move to reveal My ways. Keep in mind that My ways are above your ways. I will show you which way you are to go, but I will not always show you more than a few steps ahead on your path. If I did this, the command for you to walk by faith would not be necessary. As it is you must walk by faith that at the next turn I will be there too, showing you the next step and teaching you which choice is right for you on the next leg of our journey.

Your life is a grand adventure! Do not let the threats of danger cause you to recoil from the challenge to plow ahead. I have provided all that you need to live a victorious life in Me.

The provision and relationships that you need will meet you along the way. There is no need to horde today's provision for fear of tomorrow. Give freely, as I lead, without fear of lack.

Let go of those people and situations that are no longer producing life. Allow me to cut away those things that are dead. Do not cling to the corpses of the past. Release your past and past relationships into My loving hands. I will either bring those dead things back to life and restore them to you along the way, as I see fit, or I will bring you into new life in another way.

You must let go of what is dead. I am the God of the living.

Have no opinion as to how I am going to meet your needs. Know only that l, beyond a shadow of a doubt, am meeting all of your needs according to My riches and glory. Taste and see that I am good.

2 Corinthians 5:7; Philippians 3:13-14;
Psalm 27:8; Mark 12:27

Twenty-five

3/10/18

You are My own special treasure. You are not being rejected by others; you are being protected by Me. Your value is far greater than can be measured by the standards of fallen man, therefore I have to step in and remove those that would under esteem and misunderstand what I am doing in and through you.

Those that come against you, turn their back on you, or simply refuse to acknowledge the beauty you offer, are insignificant players in the greater scheme of what I am doing in your life during this season. At the most they are sandpaper helping to polish the precious jewel that you are; what was once heart break and agony is slowly becoming nothing more than a minor irritation as your rough edges are polished smooth to enable you to reflect my image in greater measures. At the least, they are being revealed as examples of what I do not have for you, sign posts, pointing you to wounded parts of yourself so that you can swing open the door of your heart and have Me pull out any splinters that, left wedged in, can fester and attract flies.

There is nothing accidental taking place.

The very rejection you are experiencing is on a deep level taking place because you are no longer content to eat the crumbs from under the table. Your consciousness will catch up to what the depths of your being has already rejected. A shifting is going on. A shaking. Your life will be built entirely on the Rock, a foundation that cannot be shaken.

I see you. I know you. The value I place on your life is immeasurable. I recognize your beauty and strength. I understand all the hidden and secret places in your heart that long to be sought, discovered, and known. You are being pursued. I am jealous over you and will thwart any plan that involves the enemy of your soul carrying your heart away from Me or keeping any parts of your wounds away from My healing touch.

My love is passionate and personal. All that you are experiencing right now is being filtered through My love. It is my ardent desire to ravish you and have you experience Me in a way that all other human loves will pale in comparison. A time is coming when anyone that crosses your path will only be regarded through My perfect love for you. They will fade further away in significance until their coming and going, love or rejection, honor or dishonor, will hold no power to harm or harness you. You will be completely saturated in My love, grounded on My foundation and moving in the freedom that only comes from belonging completely and irrevocably to Me.

Hebrews 12:27; Psalm 139:1-4; Exodus 20:5

Twenty-six

Do not allow the divide between what your eyes of faith see that I have prepared for you, and what your physical eyes perceive as your reality, cause you to stumble into an ungrateful attitude of heart that refuses to be comforted in the here and now.

It is My desire for you to enjoy the blessings of peace and joy that flow from an attitude of gratitude. Your dissatisfaction with what was once considered a blessing is blocking your growth. You are not yet ready to receive what you long for. I need to be able to trust your motives for desiring greater things. As it is now, your pride is evident in that you truly believe that what you have been given for this day is somehow beneath you.

You tell yourself that it is My reputation that is at stake if you do not step into greater levels of glory and provision. Examine yourself more deeply My child. Are you sure it is My reputation that you seek to protect?

Your viewpoint on some matters has been tainted by the excesses of your life and culture. Yes, even by some of the teachings in the church.

Take pride in your low position.

I am pouring out into your life, without restraint, the true riches of My Kingdom. Oh, how My heart longs for you to know and understand that I am giving you My very best for your life right in this moment and for this moment. I am Your Father, how do you fail to see this? I know that you at times feel that you lack the ability and resources to give freely. Do not limit Me and what I am doing by your own limited mindset, view of yourself, and the world around you.

Invest what you have been given completely into the lives of those that I bring to you. You will see how quickly the laws of multiplication which I have set in motion begin to manifest both spiritually and physically in your life.

The spirit of fear must be fought with a mouth that is continually filled with praise. Open your eyes and see how the forces of darkness have bound you by convincing you to believe lies about your current circumstances and Me.

Banish all vain thoughts. Leave behind all pretense by abandoning your faulty systems of measurement. You have tested My Word and found it to be true; pride comes before destruction and a haughty spirit before a fall. Walk humbly before Me every day and allow Me to lift you up when, where, how, and with whom I decide is best. This will be easy for you now.

Remind yourself daily that My thoughts are Higher than your thoughts, and My ways are greater than Your ways. I will reward your long-suffering with deep abiding joy; you have tasted it, walked in it for seasons at a time, but a time is soon coming when there will be nothing that can shake you.

I am glad that you have held on in faith to My promises. Your faith will be richly rewarded in My time.

Once again, abandon yourself to the process. Every day, with each new challenge, abandon yourself to Me. Relax your grip. Rest your troubled thoughts. Repent for the time and life resource you have wasted in petty distractions trying to make this uncomfortable season more comfortable. Embrace the uncomfortable days with the same open arms you embrace the days of comfort and you will be protected from many needless battles.

James 4:3; James 1:9; Luke 6:38; Proverbs 16:18;
1 Peter 5:6; Isaiah 55:9; Hebrews 12:27

4/22/18

Twenty-seven

My Words to you are healing and they are life. When you
open the Bible and read you are reading My love letter to you.
I have tucked away many life-giving promises in My Word.
Seek Me there; seek Me with your whole heart and you will
find Me. There are promises that I have provided to encourage you and build your faith that I am handling all the circumstances that you face. I am working to bring about the
changes and healing that your heart longs for in your own life
and the lives of your loved ones.

Give Me your attention. Focus your mind on Me and
delve into the Words that I have given you; they are life.

They will bring life to your mortal body and into the body of your
loved ones.

Speak to Me in the morning,
as you walk on your way during the
hours of your day, and as you prepare to sleep at night. Ask Me for
what you need. Do you need more
faith? Faith comes by hearing and

hearing by the Word. Meditate on My Word day and night. As you shift your focus from the problems that surround you, and the enemies that seem to be knocking at your door, you are going to have a whole new perspective, My perspective. You will find there is nothing to fear. I love you. I love those that are dear to your heart. My love is perfect and without defect. Give yourself and the ones you love completely into My hands.

Hold onto My promises. Let go of the cares and worries that are choking out the peace and joy I have given you. I give you peace that passes all understanding. It is yours right now, not tomorrow, not when healing has already manifested in the natural realm on your behalf, but right now.

I am. I am whatever it is you need Me to be. I have promised to meet all of your needs. Do you believe that I desire to meet all of your needs? Believe My Words and your prayers will prosper. Your persistence in prayer pleases Me. Deep within your heart you know that I am a rewarder of those that diligently seek Me. Your diligence will pay off. I have dispatched My angels on your behalf. Do not doubt for one instant. My ears have not been deaf to your cries for relief. My Spirit is hovering over those things which concern you and breathing My life into them. I am creating an outcome far better than you can even right now imagine.

Patiently await the appointed time of your deliverance. It will not come one minute too late. Prepare your heart by spending time with Me, and follow Me by acknowledging Me in all of your ways. I am making your path straight. I am healing those things that you are holding before Me in your heart in prayer.

No more agony. Taste and see that I am good. You will not be denied.

Proverbs 3:6, 4:22; Jeremiah 29:13; Romans 10:17; Philippians 4:19; Hebrews 11:6; Psalm 34:8

Twenty-eight

I am making streams in the desert. As you open yourself more and more to My wisdom and My ways in your life, I will open more and more doors of opportunity for you to walk through. Each place that I bring you to will be for My purposes. My purpose is your assignment. Your assignment in each situation and for each relationship and interaction will become clear to you in ways that you have yet to experience.

I am beginning to illuminate the path beneath your feet with a texture and color unlike anything you have touched or seen before. Your sleeping spirit is being awakened to the dimension of Heaven where nothing is impossible for those that believe. There is more testing ahead, but in each circumstance a glance in My direction will enable you to comprehend the lesson and be changed by it. There is nothing to fear. Stand firm in faith. Trust My ways in your life, and follow the path that I am marking beneath your feet. It will not be the path of least resistance, although you will walk it with ease if you take My hand and cast your burdens on Me the moment you feel their weight on your shoulders.

Do not pause long in mediation on how I intend to fulfill My promises to you or make your dreams come to pass. Simply ask Me what your part is daily, and do what I set in front of you to do. One step at a time, one day at a time, one lesson at a time, you will be moved forward into all that I have prepared for you. Learn to take time away; set aside time in your schedule to speak with Me and learn to quiet your thoughts so that you can hear what I have to say to you. You will be blessed beyond measure as you grow in this spiritual discipline. Each new level I bring you to will require you to have learned to draw on My strength and to lean not on your own understanding on a deeper level. When you are prepared, right on time, I will open a door to the next season of your life.

 Claim from My storehouse of blessing everything you need for each day. Do you need healing in your body? Claim it as done. Do you need financial provision? Claim it has arrived. Do you need grace to deal with difficult circumstances or people? Claim grace to cover your relationships and situations. Do you need wisdom? Claim My wisdom and understanding. Everything I have I give to you so that you can go and bear much fruit. I desire that you live a fruitful life, vibrant and pulsating with My power. You are My child and bare My image to the world. You are blessed more than you can now comprehend. I am

for you, not against you. I will make all things in your life to work together for good when you love Me.

You are called to be a part of My good purposes on the earth. Nothing can separate you from My love.

Psalm 119:105; 1 Peter 5:7; John 15:16;
Romans 8:28, 31

7/1/18

Twenty-nine

No judgement. No fear. No dread. No doubt. Walk in complete, confident assurance of My sovereignty in your life and in the world around you. No chaos. No rushing. Sit with Me in heavenly places. All rest. All trust. Give up your need to control and question. Focus your eyes on the cross. Remember that many things are not as they seem. I am setting the stage for new life. I am the Master Builder. Your view is limited; you are but one part of the whole.

There are blockages barring the flow of your purpose being fully realized and accomplished. Let nothing impede your progress. Let go of things that are behind. Keep your eyes on the prize. Bury your talent no more. Banish all thoughts of defeat and condemnation.

I died to take away the sins of the world. Take your eyes off of sin and place them on Me and the finished work of My cross; sin will lose its control over you. I died to set you free. You are free. Walk in freedom by casting out thoughts and reasoning that contradict the Truth of My Word. Stop listening to the voice of the accuser who seeks to infiltrate My

Kingdom by retaining or gaining ground in the hearts and minds of those that I have called redeemed.

There is no lack. There is nothing to worry about. Pray. Trust. Obey. One step at a time. One day at a time. March forward, taking authority over everything that I have given you. Claim. Claim. Claim. Do not give up one inch of ground in your heart to the enemy. Your heart belongs to Me. Believe this. When thoughts arise that do not spring from the fruit of My Spirit: love, joy, peace, patience, kindness, goodness, faithfulness, gentleness and self-control, know that you are dealing with arsenal from the enemy of your soul or your own flesh and cast them aside quickly. Breathe deeply, inhale the depths of My love for you and for the world and release yourself, others, and the circumstance of life into My hands of grace and justice.

Take time apart with me to rest. So many of your problems stem from your refusal to care for your mind, body, and spirit through proper nutrition and rest. Realize I do not begrudge you what is your need. I am a Good Father and delight to give My children what they need. Rest and be refreshed.

If you feel your energies are depleted, rest. If you believe you do not have time to take care of yourself in this way, you are not living the balanced life I desire for you to live. I long for you to walk with Me in peace and quiet confidence. A harried life, full of responsibilities and duties, must include ample times of rest and play. If you do not believe you have time to spare for yourself and nurturing your relationship with Me you are spending time doing some things I have not asked or required.

In the same way I have created your body to benefit from times of fasting to rest your digestive system. Seek Me for guidance on the length and type of fasting from food that I want to use in your life. You will be blessed, and become a greater blessing to others, by this discipline that I call my disciples to practice.

Come away with Me. Learn to receive from the storehouse of my goodness every day. Stop anticipating failure and defeat. I Am.

Philippians 3:13; John 1:29;
Galatians 5:1, 22-23; Matthew 9:15

Thirty

I have more blessing, provision, security, and love available to you than you can right now imagine. I am holding out My open hands and open arms to you. Come to Me and receive every good thing that you need for life and holiness. My heart is to do you good all the days of your life.

I am not holding out on you. Are you holding out on Me? Swing open the doors of your heart and life wide; invite Me to enter in. Fellowship with Me in the morning. There is much that I long to share with you: My heart toward you, My thoughts for your future, and My way that will show you the path to walk out of every tight place into a spacious place of freedom in Me and abundance in My presence. All that I have, I give to you.

Meet Me in the secret place of your spirit, where I reside, and tell Me your deepest secrets. Share with Me your fears. Cast all of your cares on Me, knowing that I care for you and am working in all the details of your life. I long for you to know Me the way that I know you. I long to hear you say that you trust Me to fulfill the promises I have given you in My Word. I am not like your earthly father. I am solid and steady, generous and gentle. I am not holding your sins against you or waiting for you to be perfect to release My blessing into your life. When you reach for Me, I am here to be grasped. You can hold onto Me; know that I am holding onto you. I desire to be in intimate, unbroken fellowship with you. I want you to share your joys and disappointments with Me. Listen for My response. Be still and know that I am God. I am your Father, a Father that will never leave you or forsake you.

Give Me your heart. Give Me your hope. Remove your expectations from those that you believe have the power to bring greater levels of provisioning into your life and place all of your expectations on Me. I will answer your prayers, but you must release into My hands the who, where, when, and how. Relax your grip and cast your care. Trust Me.

I am working day and night to bring about an outcome far greater than your limited understanding can comprehend at this time. Your part is to spend time with Me to draw your strength from Me. Spend time in My Word growing in faith. Faith comes by hearing and hearing by My Word. In this time of solitude that you set aside to get to know Me more, you will grow in wisdom, insight, and understanding. Your path will become clear beneath your feet. I will lead you into a spacious place where you will ask whatever you want and it will be done. Doubt and unbelief will be swallowed up by My glory illuminating in vivid pictures My specific promises and thoughts towards you.

Come away with Me and be transformed by the renewing of your mind. You are my child. I am pleased with you. I have good plans to prosper you and not to harm you.

1 Peter 5:7; 2 Corinthians 5:19;
Romans 10:17, 12:2

7/5/18

Thirty-one

Give Me your wandering mind as an offering of trust. Allow Me to calm the crashing waves of anxiety caused by your desire to figure out how I intend to fulfill My promises in the circumstances and relationships that are most important to you. I am giving you exactly what you need to walk forward in confident assurance that I am moving to untangle the confusion caused by your worry that I do not have your best interests at heart.

You can only see what I have shown you. I have all the information that is needed to bring about the absolute best  and highest outcome of all that concerns you. Can you see that by insisting on trying to plan every detail of your deliverance you rob yourself of the blessing that I have for you this day? Not only that, but you miss out on taking the necessary steps of preparation that I am leading you to take by spending your time gazing into the future and projecting your ideas of the best solutions to your problems onto the screen of your consciousness. This practice is filling up space that would be better occupied with faith in My goodness and loving Me, yourself, and others this day.

Be present in the here and now.

I know that you need to be encouraged to hold onto the dreams and visions that I have placed within you. I do not mind you asking for signs, wonders, and revelation that will strengthen you as you wait on Me, but on some days I am pained by your refusal to just rest when I am not showering you with My revelation knowledge.

Know that on the days when I am not dropping buckets of understanding over your mind, it is because I can see that you are already submerged in pools of 'more than enough.' I am waiting for you to open your eyes to the abundance around you and, with the joyful trust of a child, begin frolicking and playing in the springs of My favor that you are already flowing in. It saddens Me to see you straining your eyes to the sky for a drop of revelation into your future and problems solution while standing in the waters of all that I am in your life up to your neck. If you are not going to swim and play in My abundance, at least kick back and relax. Let tension and apprehension leave your soul and body. I love you! Close your eyes. Give them a rest from straining towards heaven to see what I am not ready to reveal.

Today I give you a choice: either plunge joyfully into the stream of My Spirit that surrounds you, or lean back into all that I am for you in this very moment. Let your feet leave

the ground and rest on the gentle sea of peace that passes all
understanding.

2 Corinthians 9:8; John 10:10;
Philippians 4:7

Chirty-two

My Word to you today is 'Expand.' You have felt in some areas of your life that you are stretched too thin already. The thought of expanding to make room for more may seem a daunting command. You have been given a broad view of some of the things that I have in My heart to do in your life, but the hours turn into days, the days into weeks, and it often seems like you have only been inching along. You wonder how you will ever have the time or resources to accomplish those dreams I have placed in your heart.

You have settled into a routine, taking care of your daily tasks and pouring your heart into the relationships that are important to you. I am proud of you. You take your responsibilities seriously. I know the areas of your life that you have become stuck in time and time again. I see better than you that with each round of having to deal with that stubborn stronghold resurfacing, you are recognizing that you are not as powerless over it as you had once thought. Pruning can be painful.

I know those areas of your life that you are breezing through almost effortlessly, having mastered the undertaking through perseverance and hard work. Pay attention to these areas in the coming months. I will be shifting some things around to begin to challenge your faith to operate in new realms of awareness of My Kingdom's reign here in the earth. Pray, 'Your Kingdom come. Your will be done.'

There are areas of your life that on some days you are certain you have learned the secret of being content. In other areas of your life, and on other days, you recognize you still rail against circumstances that have been allowed into your life by My sovereign hand. Sometimes you resist My ways with you simply because you do not understand what it is that I am accomplishing for you through the struggle.

I have more in mind for your life than you are right now prepared to receive. If I were to lay open your life internally, and I do in the night hours as you sleep, there would be homes, dwelling places, not fit for the habitation of a child of the God of the universe, the Creator of heaven and earth. Are you stuck living in one room, dark and gloomy, locked away from the rest of the rooms in your hearts home because of bitterness, unforgiveness, or pride? Do you have crowds of people living in the chambers of the heart, fragments of yourself manifesting characteristics and responses created to protect yourself, carry burdens, and process your pain apart from My healing touch: a mother's envy or manipulation, a father's rejection or abuse, a hedonistic aunt or uncle, a mentally unstable sibling or an old love flame? They show up in your dreams. I am showing you wounded parts of yourself in dream symbols through magnifying the traits of those that have influenced your view of Me, yourself, and the world around you.

You are none of those traits. Who you are is a redeemed and forgiven, one-of-a-kind creation, set apart and made holy by the blood of the Lamb.

Pay attention to your dreams. I want you to see where you are still wounded and settling for less than the riches of My Kingdom. I see homes crumbling from years of neglect. Tiny houses having shrunk in size because of feelings of inadequacy and unworthiness. Flooding, showing overwhelming emotions causing damage to your life. Your childhood home, taking you back to an age where you are stuck in a hidden, unhealed wound. You cannot find a home? Afford the rent? Move from place to place? What do you dream of when you dream of a house? Pay attention to what I show you in the night.

I Am your home! Live in Me and live life to the fullest. I am building a house not made of human hands. Your body is My temple and within the confines of your heart, I live. Let Me reign on the earth through your surrendered life. Let Me make you aware of the mansion I have for you; it is filled with provision. I am within you. Everything you need for an abundant life and holiness are within you. I have custom made a mansion for you. When you reside with Me there, you will know beyond doubt that no lack exists.

The Kingdom of God is within you. Seek true treasure. Look to Me; cast out every thought and theory that sets itself up against the knowledge of who I am in you. Look into the Word that gives life and find out who you really are and what

I have said about your new creature status. You are not just a conglomerate of your past and past relationships, set like a computer to react and respond to the specification of the world, the enemy, or your past conditioning. You are not of this world. You have My seed on the inside of you, filled with the DNA of heaven. The specifications of your life were created by Me. The relationships and circumstances of your life were allowed by My sovereign hand.

Like Joseph, trust and obey and be elevated, even through the hard and unfair places, from the pit to the palace!

If you surrender fully to Me and let Me into all of the rooms of your heart where I stand at the door and knock, I will come in and transform your human condition into the state of unconditional love. Our love is bound by no one and nothing. Out of Our love flows the power to move mountains and create valuable changes in the lives of those I will send to you for a healing touch. Your thoughts will be My thoughts, unimpeded by the influences that seek to hold you captive. Your words will be My Words. Whatever you speak will come to pass. Your hands and feet will move at the impulse of My love.

The rooms of your mansion will be filled with the trappings of true wealth. People will come to you from the North and from the South, from the East and from the West. They will line up to touch their lives to your life; they will want to partake in the richness of the favor and blessing that follow you wherever you go. You will lend and not borrow. Overflow is your portion.

Ramshackle houses are for slaves. Basement rooms are for servants. If you obey My commands, I have called you friends. My friends that are willing to drink from the cup from which I drink will also live as I lived on the earth, in fullness of joy and with a wealth of provision, miracle working power, and influence that reaches far beyond their immediate surroundings.

I was no magician. I only did what I saw My Father do. I only said what I heard My Father say. As I was on the earth, so shall you be.

You do not have to wait for the sweet by and by to live within your mansion in heaven. The Kingdom of heaven is here. Let Me build within your heart, on the solid foundation of your faith in Me, an elaborate dwelling place provisioned with many wonderful rooms to fellowship with Me. I will tell you great and mighty things you have not heard.

Crash, smash, and destroy all of the idols that still remain.

Let go of all that is dead, and walk in newness of life. Let nothing but the glory of My Presence be set upon the throne of your heart, My temple.

Rule and reign with Me in Life.

John 14:14, 15:2; 2 Corinthians 10:4-5;
Luke 17:21; 2 Timothy 2:12

Thirty-three

I am accelerating the work that I am doing in your circumstances. What would have taken 10 years without the added pressure of My touch will be completed in 10 months. Can you take the heat? Certainly you can! I have worked with you to increase your capacity to stand the pressure without cracking. Do not say that you cannot handle one more disappointment or one more set back. Take your expectations off of the process lining up with your need to be in control and place them onto My promise to answer your earnest and heartfelt prayers of faith.

There are no setbacks. You are experiencing set ups. Each imperfection that comes to the surface is, by its nature, going to produce feelings of angst. These emotions are only markers of what needs to be laid on the altar, guideposts of what not to carry into the future.

'What is this?!' You will think and wonder why I am not blocking the perceived intrusion on your righteousness, peace, and joy. My answer is that these are those things that are no longer useful being brought to the surface. I must remove them from your heart and life for you to move forward in My

Kingdom. Recognize that even when you see dark spot after dark spot bubbling up from the depths of your lives and relationships, My goodness is at work. Many wounds are healed in layers.

Keep your eyes open for the ways I will redeem your mistakes and the mistakes of others as you exercise audacious faith in My being your Vindicator and Redeemer. Let Me lift the burden; cast the care of your weakness onto My strong shoulders. It brings My heart delight to turn those mistakes into doorways of blessing for you and others. Receive My grace and watch it in action. Laugh in the face of the accusations of the enemy that say you have blown it.

Boldly ask Me to bless your mess.

OK, got it for yourself? Do you feel better just knowing that I have your back? Now, turn this hope outward towards those on your path that need the same faith from you to believe that I can work miracles out of their wobbly attempts at obedience and sometimes half-hearted efforts at perfection. Look deeper than the surface and wider than the day. Have they really made so little progress as you imagine?

Set yourself free from living under the microscope of scrutiny that imagines I am so small that I am unable to work all things for good. Examine your heart and life before Me, accept My rebuke, and then receive My encouragement and restoration. Remember the cross and My promise of redemption. Apply My blood to your sins and transgressions. Claim the redemption of the cross for all of life's circumstances. Let the anxiety of your imperfections, imperfect relationships, and the imperfect circumstances you find yourself in drive you closer into My heart. Do this and be changed from glory to glory. Enjoy the glory you are in!

Accept others in their current level of glory. Preach the word; be prepared in season and out of season; correct, rebuke and encourage – with great patience and careful instruction. Do not let anyone tell you that you should not try to change someone else! You are created in My image. Do not use manipulation and control- this is witchcraft. Use My Word, My Wisdom, and My Spirit. Let me change you. Let Me use you to change the world.

Malachi 3:3; Psalm 55:22; Isaiah 61:1-3; 2
Corinthians 3:18; 2 Timothy 4:2

Thirty-four

I am close to the broken-hearted and save those that are crushed in spirit. There are far greater things ahead then those things that are behind. I have been working to resolve those things that are near and dear to your heart since the moment you made up your mind to surrender them completely into My hands. I know that you have at times picked things back up and tried to wrap your mind around the possible solutions and outcomes that I could be planning, but you are right in stepping away from the problem to focus on praising Me.

Do not be afraid to face head on the conversations and changes that need to take place to extradite yourself out of those things that are at a boiling point in your life. Enough is enough. Continue to remove yourself from those things that have become intolerable and separate yourself unto Me in praise and worship. I am not requiring or asking you to stay in the fires of these afflictions. I have provided a way out. Pay no attention to the heightened anxiety or insecurities associated with climbing onto the ladder I am providing as a way out. What is presently out of reach and seems difficult to obtain is coming into focus; you need only to put your courage in Me.

There are far better things ahead than anything that is being pruned out of your life. Very truly I tell you, unless a kernel of wheat falls to the ground and dies it remains only a single seed, but if it dies, it produces many seeds.

<u>Do not be afraid to let go.</u> Your life and the joy that I have placed in you will go on, flourish, and produce a far greater yield for you having completely surrendered and died to any hope for a specific outcome. Anchor your hope securely in Me.

I do not want to waste your beauty. Do not throw your pearls before swine. I have placed flowers of thoughts bloom-

ing with life in your hair and attached ribbons of celebration on your garments to flow for others to see and know that My hand is on you. My life-giving power is within you. Your beauty is clear to Me; all that you have to offer will not be wasted. I have a good plan to restore to you the years that the locusts have eaten.

I am purifying your heart and desires and preparing you to receive more than you had hoped for. Let go of the less than you know that I have for you to make room for the good things that are ahead. You can trust Me to lead you out of all extremes into a place of balance and peace that passes all understanding. This is not an 'out of the pot and

(handwritten margin note: Wow-)

into the frying pan' transport. I am translating you from the kingdoms and systems of earth into the Kingdom of Heaven here on the earth where your deepest hearts desires will be recognized, acknowledged, and fulfilled.

Out of this acknowledgement will flow your hearts truest prayers. Once these prayers leave your lips, they will be answered in heaven to the exact specifications that I have planned to fulfill them. Leave the when, where, how, and who to Me.

Recognize those things that are not sent from My hand into your life and refuse to accept them. Stand firm in the knowledge that in trusting Me and following Me as I lead you out you will see the goodness that I have prepared for you in the land of the living.

Psalm 34:18; John 12:24; Matthew 7:6;
Joel 2:25; Psalm 27:13

The LORD is near the brokenhearted; He saves those crushed in spirit.

I assure you: Unless a grain of wheat falls to the ground and dies, it remains by itself. But if it dies, it produces a large crop.

Thirty-five

My sweet, sweet child, I know the weight that you are carrying. I long for you to cast your care on Me and let Me help you shoulder the load. It is too heavy for you to carry alone. Who in all the world can you depend on like you can depend on Me? I have said if someone forces you to go one mile, go with them two, and you have gladly done as I commanded.

You never imagined in all your hoping that what was thought to be one of the greatest gifts from My hand would demand that you climb the heights of a snow-covered mountain. You realized in triumphant wonder one day you had reached the top, only to turn around and notice you cannot see the good that has been done; you look around and assume you are stuck on the top of a mountain in a snow storm. My warmth radiating from the inside of you feels no match for the harsh and freezing conditions around you.

You look around for shelter. Come to Me; I alone can shelter you from the elements that you still believe are beyond your control. You search the outskirts of the terrain for anything you can gather to build something suitable for a fire. Yes! Look around. What do you see that you can surrender to the flames of My love? Ask Me to show you what useful thing you have to offer and, as cold as it feels, gather the things I show you and build a fire. The warmth that you seek will not be found in the hearts of your companions at this time; turn away from all distractions and give yourself fully to the task at hand.

You are faced with an icy environment, having been led a long and steep path, following the way of love. You have been led, not to the fruitful valley that you had imagined you were to find, but to a place not fit for human habitation. There were glimpses on the way building your hope for the glorious oasis you were certain was just around the next bend, but now, for days on end, you see nothing but ice.

The world can be so cold, you think. Where is the love that you seek? Where is the life that you long for? Where is the hand that you can hold in unity of mind and spirit, devoid of the cruelty of betrayal? Turn away from these questions now. Turn towards Me, the answer to all questions, and the fulfillment of all dreams. Ask Me to show you what more I want you to give. I am going to show you something completely new, something you had not thought of yet. You think, 'Give more when giving has brought me to this eerie place where without the hope in what I can imagine everything looks grey and dull?'

Do not be afraid of losing your faith. Even when you are faithless, I am faithful.

Right now, ask Me. Turn away from asking questions of those that are themselves part of your problem and ask of Me, your Solution. I do not want your love to run cold because of your surroundings. Together we will build a fire out of the more I have provided for you to give.

Do not seek to warm yourself in the embrace of those whose love knows not the warmth of My touch. In your current condition, do not feel responsible for being their source of heat. I am going to build a fire right in front of your eyes out of those things that I ask you to sacrifice to Me that will melt not only the ice and snow around you as the storm passes by, but will bring warmth to all that step on the path you are walking with Me. Look at your life. Would you hold back burning what could produce a blazing fire on the heights of a snow covered mountain when your very life depended on it?

Ask Me. I will be candid and specific. Obey, and then sit back and watch the scene change like a fast forward time-lapse of the changing of the seasons. It will be no miracle. You have been allowing the conditions to take you backwards to a time in your life when I was not known by you like I now am. I am simply going to reverse the lag created by the fear of future outcomes looking like the past.

I make all things new!

Matthew 5:41; 2 Timothy 2:13

Thirty-six

When you cling to Me when the sky is darkened, the store-houses appear empty, and your dreams seem shattered on the rocks of delay, your faith becomes mature and complete. Those of you that swallow your pride and allow yourselves to share in My humiliation, bearing your sorrows bravely, will come to know Me and experience My faithfulness to a fuller measure than those that only follow Me when I am leading them through lush meadows brimming with life.

When I ask you, will you come away with Me to pray for strength to bear the weight of what must be done to bring salvation, or will you be overcome with slumber and leave Me alone to bear the agony of the cup that I must drink to take away the sins of the world? Do not be one that turns back as I am nailed to the cross, unwilling to suffer through what is hard to comprehend as love and goodness in your own life. Why do you think it strange that you have

been led a difficult way, burdened at times to suffer through rejection and betrayal? There are only two paths along the road to Calvary: Betray and reject Me, or suffer with Me as I am betrayed and rejected.

John, the disciple that knew I loved him, in being convinced of My love, found the courage to stay with Me as I suffered and died. It was to this disciple I trusted My earthly mother into his care. And to those that come with Me all the way to the cross, to those that know that I love them and refuse to abandon Me at My hour of need, even when it appears that I am weak and powerless to save them, I will, in turn, entrust what is closest to My heart on the earth.

Come and let us move beyond the cross in your circumstances. Let us remember the tomb where My body was laid. To My disciples it seemed as if all hope had been lost. You too forget all the Words I have spoken to you about your life when you are suffering greatly in confusion, observing what is before your eyes as certain defeat. Remember My Words to you. Remember My miraculous power that saved your soul and gave you eternal life. Is anything too hard for Me? Am I a man that I should lie? Have I not told you ahead of time so that when you saw My glorious resurrection from the dead in your circumstances, you would praise My Father in heaven knowing that He has all power in heaven and on earth and Has given it to Me?

Stay close to Me; be fearless at the foot of the cross, hopeful at the mouth of the tomb, and triumphant in Me to share the news with others that you have seen the scars on My hands, feet, and side and know beyond a shadow of a doubt that I have risen from the grave.

Do not doubt My love and faithfulness while you are in the process of My resurrection power accomplishing in your circumstances all that is necessary for My purposes to be fulfilled.

I have come that you might have life and have it to the full.

Jeremiah 32:27; Numbers 23:19;
Matthew 28:18; John 10:10

Thirty-seven

Do you want to know the direction I am asking you to take but are feeling confused? Confusion does not come from Me. I am not the author of confusion. You have taken hit after hit in recent months from the enemy camp and kept your hope anchored in Me. I have taken notice of your commitment to serve Me and move at the impulse of My love.

I know how you long to know My will and make the correct decisions. You have spent a great deal of time and prayer looking for the answers. I have given you some instructions, which steps to take that are directly in front of you. For now, I am asking you to let it rest. Let your mind rest from trying to figure out exactly when and how I intend to move you forward in the coming weeks. There is nothing more that needs to be decided this week on this matter. I want you to focus all of your energies on being thankful. Trust Me and do not be afraid. The answer will come loud and clear at the precise moment I desire it to.

I love that you seek answers that I have concealed. I am veiling things for your own protection. By now you know that you can trust Me, the Way, when you cannot see far off

in the distance. I have asked you to
walk by faith. You have asked Me to
make your way clear. I have heard
your prayers and have sent forth My
Word to illuminate the path beneath
your feet. For today, and in the days
ahead, My Word to you is 'Rejoice!'
Rejoice in the peace that I have all
the details of your life figured out.
Rejoice in the truth that I love you
and have good plans to prosper you.

Prosperity is your portion. There will be no dwindling of
your resources as you have feared. Do not hold back your
offering of thanks now. I have spoken:

> Those who sow with tears
>   will reap with songs of joy.
> Those who go out weeping,
>   carrying seed to sow,
> will return with songs of joy,
>   carrying sheaves with them.

You are coming into a new season, of this you have felt
certain for some time. Do what I have placed right before
you on your path with the most excellent and diligent of
care as one awaiting their promotion. Hum and sing and
make music in your heart to Me, your Redeemer and the
Promoter of your life. Share a smile just for Me knowing
that we share secrets. What others might not fully realize,

although they are starting to suspect, is that you hold the keys to My Kingdom in your hands. Praise Me and show Me your appreciation by scattering your seed along the path where I am leading you.

1 Corinthians 4:33; Psalm 119:105;
Jeremiah 29:11; Psalm 126:5-6

Thirty-eight

1-20-19

Let Me take you in My arms and whisper to you of My great love for you. I need you to come to Me and give Me a chance to pour out My heart to you. I have stood patiently by as you have poured out your heart to Me. Will you come to Me, and give Me an opportunity to respond to your need for comfort and to your desire for deep fellowship with someone that loves you? My heart is jealous and protective over you. Will you let Me in? Will you change your schedule to make more time for Me? Thoughts of you are always before Me, how I can make all decisions, both yours and others, right or wrong, to work together for your good. Climb into My lap and let us discuss your life, your feelings, your thoughts, your hopes and dreams. Yes, speak to Me even about your fears and disappointments. When you open your eyes in the morning, immediately breathe My name and ask Me to wrap My arms around you. I will take the weight of whatever comes your way and shoulder the load.

There is much that I want to impart to you. I have infinite wisdom and insight into the inner workings of all that pertains to you and those that you love. Nothing is a surprise to Me! All the days of your life are written in My book.

I want to teach you how to get everything you need from Me, the One that has the whole world in My hands. My love for you is personal and powerful. My love for you is passionate. My love and Presence can be as tangible as you want them to be. I am not far off from you. I am here, standing at the door of your heart and life, knocking. Let Me come into every room. I want to infuse every aspect of your life with My palpable Presence.

I want you to carve out more time just to climb into My lap with no distractions. Focus your mind on Me by beginning to thank Me. I am there for you working on everything that concerns you. I am comforted by My children when they vocalize their faith in My character. It hurts My heart when you imagine I am withholding from you what love requires. If I did not spare My own Son on your behalf, how can you imagine I am now punishing you for your imperfections? I am working through all the details of your life to bring you to Myself. In Me is the life that you long for. There is no life to be found elsewhere. I created you for Myself.

How can you still feel neglected and forgotten? You are on My mind night and day. I never sleep or slumber. Close your eyes and imagine Me sitting and waiting in anticipation for the time you set aside to fellowship with Me. Imagine how it feels to Me when you refuse to create space in your life to spend time alone with Me. I understand what it feels like to be neglected and forgotten. Let us come together daily and meet each other's desire to be known and loved, sought and cherished.

No one will ever know and understand you as I do. Deep calls to deep.

Romans 8:28; Revelation 3:20;
John 1:4 Psalm 42:7

4/24/19

Thirty-nine

You ask Me in faith and then waiver at your own audacity. It is no matter. I love that you have asked at all. One does not make the effort to ask of Someone that they do not on some level believe has, not only the ability, but the desire to deliver the goods that are sought. I will move Heaven and earth to confirm My will and to provide the provision to accomplish My will through the life of one of My surrendered children. Trust and do not be afraid. Be strong and courageous. Come boldly to the throne with your requests.

Go ahead and put out your fleece. Pay attention to the people and circumstances I am putting in your path. Walk in love. When you step out to serve, listen to, or support someone that may not seem to have anything to offer back, it can lead you to the very door of opportunity or confirmation that you have been praying to find. Stop checking on your obvious sources of support to measure how certain your victory will be. Instead busy yourself with My interest in other people. Stop seeing every unexpected turn in the road as an obstacle to your desires being realized and grow up into a faith that understands the intricate pattern for good that I am weaving out of all things that I allow into your life.

Once you begin to be more fully convinced of My directions, do not be surprised when I begin to stack the odds against you in the natural realm. Many of my children refuse to allow Me to remove crutches, while at the same time praying for My miracle working power to flow through their lives. Why waste time fighting to hang onto those things that have no power to save? No more lamenting the loss of what I am filtering out of your life, those things and people that provide false security.

Do you want to fly? In My Kingdom there is only one way to accomplish this impossible feat. It will not be from the safety of the ground, felt firmly beneath your feet, that you will take off and begin to soar. Cut your earth ties. Climb the heights of the mountain. Walk to the edge. Wait for My timing. Listen for My command. When you hear Me clearly say, 'This is the Way. This is the time,' jump! You will be lifted up on wings of faith delivered from the laws of nature that laugh in the face of all that I have promised to accomplish in and through your life.

Joshua 1:9; Hebrews 4:16; Judges 6:37;
Isaiah 30:21

Forty

There is much that I want to say to you that you are not yet ready to hear. Can you move forward in faith and trust Me with the loose ends? Take My hand; do not be afraid. You are concerned that you do not know the way that you are to go, but there is no need for concern; I am the Way. I am standing right beside you. Just take My hand and follow Me.

Imagine the savory tastes of the most delicious foods you have dined on, the fondest childhood memory you can conjure up in your mind's eye, and the exhilaration that you felt during your most memorable life adventure. Do you remember the emotions you experienced while reading an exceptional story or watching a breathtaking scene from a movie? Can you recall the butterflies in your stomach when spending time with a human companion that is near and dear to your heart? And music, have you heard the sound of Heaven come vaguely through a melodious symphony? What about the inspiration and beauty you flow in while watching dancers, looking at masterfully created sculptures and paintings, or co-creating with Me by making or performing your own art? Close your eyes and meditate on these things.

These things are not Me; they are doorways into the place of My heart where your deepest needs will be met. These experiences are nothing more than a longing that is stirred, a surface that is scratched; your face is pressed against the glass and you have glimpsed the splendor of the Kingdom of Heaven. In My heart, in My arms, in My Kingdom, your mouth will eat and be fully satisfied, your eyes will look and behold a vast expanse of all that is beautiful blocking the view of all darkness and ugliness, your ears will hear the chorus of the angels singing, "Holy, Holy, Holy is the Lord God almighty." You will join in sweet abandon to the worship welling up from your heart and flowing out towards My throne.

It is in My Kingdom that you will encounter My Presence. Although your yet to be transformed human body has not the capacity to contain all that I am, at the appointed time, I will come for you and take you to be with Me in the home that I am preparing for you. I will give you a new and glorious body, untainted by sin and death. The new body I give you will be able to contain My glory in a measure beyond anything you can now imagine. You and I will be united forever in glorious ecstasy.

Seek My face good and faithful servant. Seek Me with your whole heart while I can be found. Ask to be filled with Holy Spirit to the greatest capacity available to your mortal body. Your body is My temple on the earth. Do not be afraid to be crushed by the weight of My glory.

Do not fret about where I am leading you or how you are being led. I am the Creator and King of the universe! All of the days of your life are written in My book. I do not exist in time as you do. Take My hand. Walk by faith. Savor the taste of glory that I am giving you. Remember you are not home yet.

John 14:6; Isaiah 6:3; John 14:3; 1
Corinthians 15:44; Psalm 139:16

Forty-one

Fear no evil, not because evil does not exist or is not a threat to your life and progress, but because I am. I am good. I am for you. I am sovereign over your circumstances. Trust Me. I am not trembling at the thought of all that you are facing, wondering how in the world we will overcome the mounting obstacles. Do you know that some of the very things that you are panicking over I have allowed into your life because it pleases Me to see My children trusting Me in the face of the impossible?

I know the beginning from the end. Change your perspective and change your life. Look at everything, every single thing, that is allowed in your life from My perspective. Take a stand against the forces of evil that are coming against all that I have promised you by bold and steadfast confidence in prayer. Relinquish your need to control other people and your tendency to try and have it all figured out, which is just another way to give yourself the illusion of being in control. Let it be enough for you to know that I am in control; trust that I have your best interests at heart.

Free yourself from the prison of your sentiment that imagines the way things are coming together, or falling apart as you often believe, are some random series of events that are leading to failure and more heartbreak.

Lighten up My precious child. In this world you will have trouble and suffering, but take courage- I have overcome the world. What does this mean for you in the here and now? It means that you are to believe wholeheartedly that I am working ALL things for your good if you love Me. Focus on loving Me and let Me work all things for your good and My glory. Your joy should not hinge on specific outcomes or certain people. Do not set yourself up as a sitting duck for the enemy by allowing anything to become an idol in your life.

You may not believe yourself to be practicing idolatry, but if you are unable to experience My love, peace, and joy when things are not going the way your opinions says they ought to, you are showing Me that you have placed your trust and hope in something or someone other than Me. Renounce your idols and come boldly to the throne of grace asking Me to give you fresh eyes to see the abundant life I died for you to have already in your lap today, not tomorrow, not in the sweet by and by, not when your desired outcomes have been realized, but right this very moment.

Pause and breathe in the breath of life. Release your need to understand every detail of how I am moving on your behalf. Trust Me and obey Me. Keep your eyes fixed on My Words and My face. Take My hand and step out boldly into the day eager to do My will in all things. Leave your preconceived ideas and opinions of what My goodness should look like behind. Hold everything and everyone loosely. Nothing else is needed for your fulfillment but to know Me. I do not tire of reminding you to seek first My Kingdom and My righteousness and all of these things will be added to you as well.

I am a generous Father. I am not holding out on you.

Psalm 103:19; Isaiah 46:10; John 16:33;
Matthew 6:33

Forty-two

Why are you so downcast My precious child? Where is your faith in My love and hope for My future grace to come through for you? Please continue to trust Me in spite of the hurt inside. There is nothing that you can not accomplish if you will believe. Do not focus on the stench of the rotting flesh or mourn the death of your dreams as if I am powerless over your circumstances. I have not ceased from maneuvering, by My Spirit, all of the pieces to the puzzle of your life, to fit them together into My perfect design. I know there is confusion as to how I will arrange things in your favor. Many of the pieces are shaped in such a way that they do not match the space in which you believe they are to go. Stop trying to shove a square into a circle and step back in order to gain a new perspective of the overall picture.

You ask Me, "What can I do?' My answer is that you must surrender your burdens to Me; cast your cares onto My capable shoulders and fear not knowing that I am with you and for you.

You have not yet been given some of the strategic pieces that will be needed to build onto what has already been fitted together. Calm down and stop searching for something that I have yet to give. For today, quiet yourself in My Presence and refuse to bow your knee to fear. Give Me the sacrifice of your praise and it will lift you out of the pit of self-pity, confusion, and doubt. Let Me deliver you from the enemies plan to lead you into despair by releasing the need to figure out how I am creating the masterpiece that is your dreams fulfillment out of the individual parts of the whole.

Change the lens you are viewing your relationships and circumstances through to take in a wider view. You are focusing on two fragmented sections that are misaligned, not taking into consideration that to everything there is a season and a purpose for everything under the sun. When the clock strikes the eleventh hour I will release the missing piece, bringing into focus the importance of calculating what was formerly thought an undesirable extraneous variable.

I know the beginning from the end. Do not let your emotions run you over and distract you from the tasks I have given you to do this day. If the enemy is unable to tempt you to leave your post, or stop your race, he is perfectly content to cause you to procrastinate your progress. Fight your battles, but fight them bravely from a posture of certain victory. Do not give the enemy the satisfaction of blowing your emotions up in your own face. By your calm posture of assurance he will cower, knowing his days of wreaking havoc in your life are numbered.

1 Peter 5:7; Hebrews 13:15; Ecclesiastes 3:1

Forty-three

Now is the time to press forward in steadfast confidence shaking off all doubt and unbelief, praying through all fear, and declaring My Word over every relative that you have been claiming will rise up and step into the light of My salvation. Many of My chosen ones have been bound in darkness and defeat, caught in webs of deceit that have tied their minds up in confusion and torment. There are loved ones that are standing at the mouth of an open grave, one step further away from Me and they will be swallowed by eternal death. I am saving the eternal lives of loved ones on the edge of physical death. I will snatch them out of the hands of the enemy and translate them into the Kingdom of light. This is the time to claim My salvation in their lives. Claim them for Me. Stand in the gap and declare their freedom from darkness.

Many of My lost children have squandered their inheritance and are eating with the pigs. Do not wait for them to return to Me of their own accord. Go get them, tell them that I am longing for them to return to Me. Invite them to come home, let them know of the banquet that I am preparing for them. Do not be like the elder brother that resents My loving kindness and mercy, refusing to give up a share of his inheritance because another of My beloved children has spent theirs on worthless pursuits. My supply is limitless. Never fear lack, it will keep you from giving out of the abundance of My provision. Everything I have is yours; will you not share with your brother the love and care I have so freely poured out on you as you have stayed by My side? Stay close to My heart by sharing My burden for My lost sheep.

Humble yourself and take on the role of a servant in My Kingdom and I will elevate you into the position of My friend. You are My friends if you do what I command. I no longer call you servants; a servant does not know his Master's business. On your finger I will place My signet ring as a sign that you are an ambassador for the King of the universe. I give you My authority to snatch back My children from the hands of My enemies. My command is to love one another as I have loved you. I have appointed you and chosen you to go and bear fruit-fruit that will last, so that whatever you ask in My name will be given to you. Ask for the lives of My lost children and watch in amazement as I turn their hearts and lives back to Me.

Today is the day of salvation!

Luke 15:11-32; John 15:14-16

Forty-four

I have given you power. Within you resides the power to have an abundant life. What you choose to focus your attention on will be magnified in its power over you. Focus your attention on Me, the only safe option. Anything else that you allow to control you will destroy you. When you fix your eyes on the unseen realm, instead of staring at the painful circumstances or lack that you are experiencing in the natural realm, you will find that abundance is the truth.

I understand the way you feel when you are in agonizing pain at the hands of those that do not recognize who you are or understand what they do and when you struggle against temptation wondering where I am in the midst of it all. I do. I will show you the way if you will follow Me.

Yes, there is a time to mourn, but there is also a time to dance. Rise up by putting a song of praise in your heart and My Words in your mouth. Stand firm in the liberty I give you by setting your mind on My Spirit; it will bring life and peace to you. Train your mind not to settle around the issues in your life that you are believing Me to change.

As a foreman studies the construction plans and gathers the building materials in preparation for creating what has been given to him in blue prints, so should you dig into My Word and apply it to your life. Why stand beside the half-finished project wailing that you do not have all that you need to finish? Did you not consider the cost of following Me, as I instructed, before you set to work? It will cost you everything. If you have lack, it is not on My end. What are you holding back from Me? I am the One that created the blue print for your life and it is I that have promised to be the Author and the Finisher. I have given you everything you need to complete the project I designed. I will provide every tool, every material, and every helper that is needed.

If you are focusing your attention on point A, instead of on Me, you can miss hearing Me say what you need is at point B. Keep moving forward towards Me in love and trust.

Many of you are unable to receive what you need for the next step of the project because your hands are full of the stuff of life I have told you to take your hands off of. Let it go in order to receive from Me. I assure you, none of the lack you are experiencing is from My hands. I give life abundant and everything that is needed to accomplish all that I have commissioned you to do.

Check the blue print, make sure it is My Word. Check the foundation, make sure it is My life. Check your life, make sure you are holding nothing back. Your pain does not come from Me.

John 12:26; Ecclesiastes 3:4; Hebrews 12:2

Forty-five

Do not worry about anything. This command seems simple enough, but to those of My children that need to have it all figured out, to the ones that are leaning on their own understanding, how to obey in this area is lost on them. I am a God that shines a light into the darkness. I bring those things that are hidden into the light. The story that I am writing is an unfolding one. I lead you with My Word. I light the path beneath your feet, sometimes only a few steps at a time. I do this so that you will not be as prone to go running out ahead of Me, or to shrink back in fear when you try to receive grace for tomorrows portion, which I will never give you today. Take My hand and have no fear.

I have given you a map, an outline of the way you are to go. I obscure many of the details in order that you will learn to walk by faith. Ponder and pray; meditate and seek, and then rest your weary mind by focusing on My great love for you. I love you. I love you. I love you. I am working tirelessly to do you good all of the days of your life. Read the signposts that I place along your path, staying open to the many ways I choose to guide you with My strong hand of favor upon you.

Stop thinking of your circumstances as good or bad. Raise your level of awareness above the shackles of the earth, high above the limited mind-set that still thinks in terms of punishment and boundaries created by sin and death. My Spirit in you elevates you beyond the natural realm into the Kingdom of Heaven, which is already among you. My heart longs for you to understand Me as I am. When you see Me as I am, you will never see yourself, others, or circumstances the same way again. Focus on Me and magnify Me in your life. Be aware that whatever you focus on will be magnified.

Stop allowing yourself to be disappointed. If I laid out your life before you and explained what I was trying to accomplish through each situation would you put your hope and trust in Me alone? There would then be no discovery, no adventure, and no need for you to constantly communicate with Me, your Guide. I want a relationship with you. Do you not yet realize that this is central to the reason I created you. It is your first purpose. I created you for Myself. I want you and long for intimacy with you. Put all your hopes in Me and they will not be disappointed.

I have told you that if you delight yourself in Me, I will give you the desires of your heart. This is the truth. Know this however, the deepest desires of your heart can only fully be interpreted through My perfect Mind. Untie My hands from moving on your behalf by trusting the specifics of your desires fulfillment into My hand. I have already told you I have more than you can imagine in the works. You know in part and prophecy in part. Only I have it all figured out.

I have said this before and will say it again, hold tightly only to Me. Anxiety is a sign you are clinging to the wrong thing. Relax your grip and enjoy your life. I have got you.

Phillipians 4:6; 2 Corinthians 4:6

Forty-six

I am the God of all comfort. Come closer My child. I am your Father and My arms long to hold you close in response to your need to be held safe and secure against the storms of your life. Why stand back from Me shivering in the cold because of your nakedness? I have a robe of righteousness designed to fit your exact measurements. Come to Me with the expectation that I am a responsible and loving Parent. I will provide for your every need. Your greatest need right now is to receive this brilliant robe of righteousness that has your name on it from My outstretched hands.

Do not be afraid of the light that shines forth into the dark places. You are safe. My light searches out what is deep and hidden to expose those things that no longer serve a purpose in your life and causes them to dissipate from the places where they have been lingering and affecting your perception of yourself, others, and My love.

Where there is injury, I bring healing. When you have lingering resentments, I pour out the grace that is needed to forgive. I am a God of justice, and I am balancing the scales. Realize My mercy and goodness are following you. Tip the scales of justice in your favor by allowing My extravagant grace to flow through you to others. With the same measure you use it will be measured back to you.

This very day I am making you My signet ring. I am bestowing this authority upon you because you have honored My name. What you decree will be established. Rise up in My power and  take possession of those things I have promised you. Let the words you speak be the words I am placing in your mouth.

According to your faith and words it will happen.

Do not fear you want too much, but take heed lest your doubts and insecurities rob you of the abundant life I have promised you.

2 Corinthians 1:3; Isaiah 61:10; Psalm 23:6, 89:14; Matthew 7:2

Forty-seven

Be patient My sweet child. I know it feels that you have had your patience tested to the uttermost limit and that you can not take one more moment of holding steady. I am giving you a most excellent gift. I am producing in you steadfast endurance and My perfect peace.

Open your eyes and see the beam of light surrounding you, cocooning you in My radiance and love. By an act of your will imagine all of the fragments of disappointment and evidence of less than My best for you pressed outward, away from the atmosphere around your spirit. Watch the fog that dulls My light pass through the membrane of My Protective covering that surrounds you.

Now My light can shine brightly unhindered by that rubbish and unimpeded by the lies that your circumstances have rendered into your mood. Today I am giving you joy. Let joy set the tone of your perception this day. Step back, out of time, knowing that all is well. I am at work.

Raise your level of expectation. Yes, even higher. Yes, against all odds. Yes, in spite of what appears to be set backs. Place all of your expectations on Me and My redemptive plan for your life. I am your Redeemer and the lifter of your head. Look up!

Take your hands off the wheel and your numbers out of the equation. I am taking you to a place that your hands can not take you, a place you have never been and do not know the way to. I am working out the answers to your problems using calculations you know nothing about. There are variables that are far above your head.

Release the need to have an illusion of control. Stop trying to help Me. I do not need your help. You need only to fully surrender yourself to the process by which I am forming you into the image of My son.

I am making all of your dreams come true. Rest in the light of My Presence and in the strength of My joy. I have got this! I have got you! There is nothing to worry about. Follow Me.

James 1:3; 2 Corinthians 3:18; John 15:11;
Nehemiah 8:10

Forty-eight

Let Me take over from here. Your anger is an indication that you are feeling the weight of the injustice of your circumstances but are refusing to trust Me to balance the scales. If you had the ability to fix your problems and your life you would not feel your need for Me. It is time to back away from the people that are unwilling to respond to the truth that I have revealed through you. Let Me show you when emotional, mental, and physical distance are needed and refuse to cling in the hopes that you can bridge the intimacy breach with your own strength and charm.

I have a plan. For now My plan is to fill up the gaps in your life and heart with My love and grace. Let Me love on you and show you My extravagant grace. It is not selfish to pull away when you feel your life force is being zapped by toiling among the thorns. You are to allow your life to be broken bread and poured out wine by carefully following the leading of My Spirit. You must relinquish control by allowing Me to lead you away from parched places and into the oasis of My Presence.

You are in a battle. Follow My command to pull back and regroup; listen for a change of plans in how to proceed. Do not be afraid to step out of the status quo. You owe no man anything but a continued debt of love. Know that at times, true love requires you to press on towards the cross alone. Though none go with you, still you must follow. Your true life companions will meet you along the way. Come alone with Me. What is it to you what I do with another? You must follow Me.

Psalm 33:5; Ephesians 1:6; Colossians 1:24;
Romans 13:8; John 21:22

Forty-nine

Prepare yourself for the time is coming, and is already here, when your faith becomes sight. Put aside your sighing and weeping; begin to praise Me for the victory that has been won. This very day I am throwing into confusion the forces of darkness that have come against you and the promises that I have placed in your heart.

Pay no attention to the commotion of your enemies clamor. Allow no unforgiveness to cling to your heart. Refuse to let yourself become bitter and hardened by the things that have come against you. Know that what has transpired was allowed to establish the boundary lines I have placed around you.

I am healing your wounds and leaving only scars as a symbol of My miracle working power that is at work in your life. Do not believe the voices coming out of the shadows that tell you that your wounds are permanent, evidence that I can not be trusted. Wait in My Presence, fully expecting to receive total restoration of your battle weary heart. I have given you a heart of flesh that beats for Love and refuses to let go of hope. Your hopes are not being disappointed. Your desires are being refined. Do not allow your dreams to be diminished by the passing of time and the disorderly way that life goes on around you.

Trust in My perfect understanding; rest in the knowledge that My ways are above your ways. This battle is not yours. Move forward with songs of praise and thoughts of thanksgiving. Clap your hands, applauding heavens bounty being released on behalf of My Kingdom manifesting itself on earth. There is a layer of debris from doubt that is being cleared out by your assurance of My power at work in your life. Watch the dust settle before your eyes as those things that have come against your promises destroy themselves by My hand leaving more spoil than you can carry off in one day.

You are convinced that this victory you wait for is far off in the distance. I tell you now that victory is today. Today is the day of salvation. The substance of what you hope for is in your hands. Let your faith rise. Plunge your hands into the storehouse of My abundant Presence and take from Me all that you need for this day. You do not have to wait for tomorrow to receive what you have need of this day. Trust that I want to lavish upon you all that you need for today.

Take your eyes off the enemy and focus your eyes on Me. I will give you a heavenly perspective. I give you righteousness, peace, and joy today. I give you healing today. I give you provision for today. All those things that were sent to harm you are sabotaged and rendered powerless by your faith and praise. Little by little I am giving your promised land into your hands. Go forth in praise and begin to glean the fields of your fallen adversaries.

Isaiah 55:8; 2 Chronicles 20:15; Hebrews 11:1; 2 Corinthians 6:2

Fifty

I want to show you something that you can see no other way but to set apart time to be alone with Me. Let Me teach you how to have visions in the day that will reveal deep and hidden things, give you direction, and bolster your faith in My unfathomable ways. My revelation knowledge is not just for prophets and seers; it is available for all My children that are filled with My Spirit and have eyes to see and ears to hear. I want our communication to be a two way flow.

Many of My children pour out their heart to Me and walk away having not taken the time to receive My response. Some are content to only feel My Presence. Some find their comfort in hearing My Word. Yes, I want you to feel Me in your emotions and hear My Words written in Holy scripture, but if you are listening with your spiritual ears you will also hear Me in the voice of My prophets, music, the sound of laughter, the cry of a baby, or the purr of a cat. Listen with spiritual ears to hear My specific Words to you; I will speak to you in dreams, visions, signs, and wonders. I want to open your eyes to how I express Myself to you in the beauty all around you. All of your senses are to be engaged in communication with Me.

How often do you partake of My flesh and My blood as I told My disciples to do in remembrance of Me? I desire even your taste buds to be used in your communion with Me. Find a quiet place with no outside distractions and enter My gates with thanksgiving and My courts with praise. Confess your sins to Me and receive My grace and forgiveness. Drink the cup and eat the bread in remembrance of Me. Do this in your homes. Do this often. Come confidently before My throne with your requests. Share your thoughts with Me and wait before Me with an open heart, mind, eyes, and ears, boldly believing I am and that I am ready and willing to communicate My thoughts to you.

Ask Me a question. Write it down. Now, put your pen to paper and write what you hear Me speak in return. Do not be afraid. Just begin to write.

Ask Me a question. Close your eyes. Watch. Let your mind rest. Trust in My ability to show you a picture or vision that I will then help you decipher as you mediate on Me. Write it down. Perhaps the revelation will be immediately revealed. Perhaps you are to seek its meaning out by watching and waiting for clues.

Enjoy your internal life lived alone with Me; be always open and waiting for what more I will reveal of Myself to you.

Meditate on My Words. Ponder My ways. Connect yourself to and learn from anointed ministers of the gospel: prophets, preachers, teachers, apostles, and evangelists.

Seek Me with all of your heart while I can be found. Allow Me to make you into the image of My Son through constant contact with Me.

Acts 2:17; 1 Corinthians 14:1; Luke 22:19; Joshua 1:8

Fifty-one

You are no longer to live under the curse of sin and death. The enemy of your soul has worn grooves in your consciousness through your past experiences that contradict the verdict I have spoken over your life. You are forgiven and redeemed, delivered from the kingdom of darkness into My glorious kingdom of light. You are called, chosen, and dearly loved. I have an inheritance for you stored up in heaven. You are My heir. I am the Creator of the universe and everything in it. My supply is unlimited.

I know that your soul has travailed in prayer and you have endured much grief as you grappled with the truth of My Word to supply all your need in light of your current

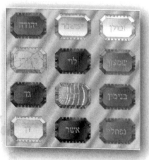

reality. I am removing your blinders, shaking all things which can be shaken until only what can not be shaken remains. It is no coincidence that what you are experiencing is unearthing the fears that still grip you and hold you immobile.

I desire that My truth permeate every memory, every motive, every hope, and every dream until it has unraveled all that ties you to being moved by reality away from the steadfast confidence that is necessary to alter those things in your life that are bowing down to anything other than My Word and My perfect will.

The enemy of your soul, and often your own subconscious, conspire together against the abundant life that is yours. Life to the full and overflowing is yours as an heir of salvation. Recognize that where there is lack and darkness in your life I am standing, waiting for the door to be opened. I want to flood those areas with My light and love. Thank Me in all things, knowing that I am exposing blockages to My Spirit and My healing power flowing into the depths of your being. I am making your broken places whole, your crooked places straight, and the places where your life is barren fruitful. Come take part in the great exchange.

Open your mouth wide and I will fill it with good things to eat. Open your mouth wide and speak My Word. Speak My will. You are not an orphan. Your Father is not impoverished or stingy. Why lament the loss of days gone by when your best days are yet in front of you? What I have for you is not far off in the distance. Do you know what it is that your heart truly desires? Do you believe I have placed that desire burning in your chest?

I am setting My children in families. I am ordaining covenant marriages. I am sending My angels to deliver vials of healing balm to cure your sickness and disease. Right now I have stamped houses 'sold' and written your name on the contract. Financial provision is being released among My people to pay off debt, build businesses, start ministries, and live a life of excellence. Choose this day to believe that your life Upgrade is My delight. It is My pleasure to do you good.

Galatians 3:13, Colossians 1:13; Romans 8:17;
Isaiah 45:2; Psalm 81:10

Fifty-two

I know there has been quite an abundance of what appears to be false starts to your assignments, tepid responses to your faith-filled prayers, and inadequate growth of the seeds you have planted. You are looking at todays' conditions as if what can be measured by your mind is the outcome of your confidence. Place your confidence more fully on Me and My promises.

Now is the season I am launching you into the assignments of heaven allocated for you. If you are being moved by your circumstances to doubt that I will answer your prayers, step up higher and enter the fire of My Spirit. Allow My passionate love to consume your reservations that have you holding back from Me your whole heart. Courageously step into the heat and allow it to burn off the dross of your hesitation.

Your harvest has arrived. You have many fields and many crops. You are focusing on the wrong field, a field that is not yet in season and neglecting to go forth in excitement to gather the abundant overflow of the crops that have fully matured. You will need helpers to carry in the overflowing baskets of My provision. Understand this, if you have sown in every season, you will reap in every season. Continue to sow into your next seasons harvest but do not neglect to act in this season to tend the seed that has already been sown.

In prayer and in diligence do the work, trusting that My hand of provision is always full and reaching out to you. Ask Me to open your eyes to what you have overlooked.

Watch as I lay at your feet the long awaited answer to your prayers. There have not been false starts; there have been needed lessons in order to prepare you for the take-off that is upon you. There are rocket ship launch times on the horizon. The testing and the test runs where necessary to prepare you to captain the ship into the new territories that I am bringing you into at the appointed time. Shake off the shackles of mis-understanding My purpose in your trial runs. They were not mistakes. I have worked out the kinks that would sabotage your unveiling strategically.

Do not cling to the past or linger long over the memories of days gone by as if they represent where I am taking you or how far you will go. What was, will never be again. Where you are going, I alone know the way and am leading you with My strong hand of power and favor moving on your behalf to clear the path. There is no lack. There is no one that has the ability to abort this process that is leading to the best outcome but you. Let go of the false notion that anyone else is standing in your way. Pack your bags, leaving behind all the pointless clutter of yesterday, and focus on the task at hand.

You have been handpicked for this mission. You have been trained. Drop the false humility; your lack of confidence does not please Me. I have chosen you, justified you, and equipped you  for My purposes to be fulfilled through your life. Stand up and command the spirits of darkness that have come against you to cease and desist. You are no longer to doubt Me or doubt yourself. What I have promised you is coming to pass. Enough of the holding back. Leave behind all that is no longer serving My purposes for your life and step into the future that I have prepared for you today.

Psalm 118:8; Isaiah 48:10; Philippians 3:13;
Romans 8:30